COUNTRIES 🌍 OF THE WORLD

Malaysia

Gareth Stevens Publishing
A WORLD ALMANAC EDUCATION GROUP COMPANY

About the Author: Anand Radhakrishnan was born in Peninsular Malaysia and brought up in the forests of Borneo. His family then moved to a city on the peninsula. After college, he returned to Borneo to carry out research on malaria. During this time, he got to carry a baby orangutan, visit a longhouse, and learn how to scuba dive. Currently finishing his doctorate in Germany, Anand awaits the day when he can return to his beloved island.

PICTURE CREDITS
Agence France Presse: 15 (center), 15 (bottom), 64, 76
ANA Press Agency: 30, 43, 72
Arkib Negara Malaysia: 15 (top)
Art Directors & TRIP Photo Library: cover, 3 (top), 6, 8 (top), 12, 16, 20, 31, 39, 40 (both), 42, 44 (top), 52, 54, 55, 61, 62, 63, 68 (top), 69 (top)
Jailani Basari: 47
Bes Stock: 4, 5, 17
Gajahtakraw Ind. Sdn. Bhd.: 70 (both)
Getty Images: 77, 81, 83, 84, 85
Haga Library Inc.: 50
Nor Sidah Haron: 46
HBL Network Photo Agency: 1, 3 (center), 7, 8 (bottom), 14, 19, 26 (top), 27, 28, 34, 35, 37, 38, 45, 48, 49, 53, 60 (top), 67, 69 (bottom), 74, 78, 79, 91
The Hutchison Library: 80
John R. Jones: 21
Earl Kowall: 2, 11, 18, 22, 32, 36, 57, 66, 68 (bottom), 75
Lonely Planet Images: 9
Malaysia Tourism Promotion Board: 44 (bottom), 51, 60 (bottom), 73
Photobank: 23, 26 (bottom), 33, 41, 56
David Portnoy: 24, 25
Purdue University Malaysian Students Association: 82
Sarawak Museum: 10
Shaw Organisation: 3 (bottom), 58, 59
Singapore SepakTakraw Federation: 71
Times Editions: 13, 29
Topfoto: 65

Digital Scanning by Digital Colour Works Pte Ltd

Written by
ANAND RADHAKRISHNAN

Edited by
LYDIA LEONG

Edited in the U.S. by
GUS GEDATUS
BETSY RASMUSSEN

Designed by
JAILANI BASARI

Picture research by
SUSAN JANE MANUEL

First published in North America in 2003 by
Gareth Stevens Publishing
A World Almanac Education Group Company
330 West Olive Street, Suite 100
Milwaukee, Wisconsin 53212 USA

Please visit our web site at
www.garethstevens.com
For a free color catalog describing
Gareth Stevens Publishing's list of high-quality
books and multimedia programs, call
1-800-542-2595 (USA) or 1-800-387-3178 (Canada).
Gareth Stevens Publishing's fax: (414) 332-3567.

© TIMES MEDIA PRIVATE LIMITED 2003
Originated and designed by
Times Editions
An imprint of Times Media Private Limited
A member of the Times Publishing Group
Times Centre, 1 New Industrial Road
Singapore 536196
http://www.timesone.com.sg/te

Library of Congress Cataloging-in-Publication Data
Radhakrishnan, Anand.
Malaysia / by Anand Radhakrishnan.
p. cm. — (Countries of the world)
Summary: An overview of Malaysia that includes information on geography, history, government, language, culture, and current issues.
Includes bibliographical references and index.
ISBN 0-8368-2360-5 (lib. bdg.)
1. Malaysia — Juvenile literature. [1. Malaysia.] I. Title.
II. Countries of the world (Milwaukee, Wis.)
DS592.R18   2003
959.5—dc21   2002026913

Printed in Malaysia

1 2 3 4 5 6 7 8 9 07 06 05 04 03

Contents

AN OVERVIEW OF MALAYSIA

Malaysia is located in the center of Southeast Asia. From the early sixteenth century until its independence in 1957, the country was ruled by three different empires — Portuguese, Dutch, and British. The British ruled Malaya (now Malaysia) the longest, from the late eighteenth century to the mid-twentieth century. As a result of Malaysia's diversified history, the country today is a melting pot of many races. While the various ethnic groups continue to observe their own cultures, traditions, and customs, they have also interacted to create a colorful heritage that is uniquely Malaysian.

Opposite: **Malaysian children enjoy bicycling and kite flying.**

Below: **These three Malay boys are dressed in traditional Malay clothing.**

THE FLAG OF MALAYSIA

The Malaysian flag has fourteen red and white stripes that represent the equal membership of the thirteen states and the federal government. The dark blue rectangle and fourteen-point star represent unity. The crescent is the symbol of Islam, and yellow is the official color of Malaysian royalty. The original flag had eleven stripes and an eleven-point star. It was first unveiled in 1950. The new flag was introduced when Singapore, Sabah, and Sarawak joined Malaya in 1963. When Singapore gained independence in 1965, the fourteenth stripe and the fourteenth point of the star were retained to represent Malaysia's capital, Kuala Lumpur.

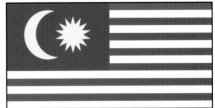

Geography

Malaysia is made up of two distinct regions — Peninsular Malaysia (or West Malaysia) and East Malaysia. Thailand borders the peninsula to the north, while Singapore lies at its southern tip. The peninsula is home to the eleven states of Johor, Melaka, Negeri Sembilan, Selangor, Pahang, Kelantan, Terengganu, Kedah, Perlis, Perak, and Penang. East Malaysia consists of the two states of Sabah and Sarawak and is found on the island of Borneo.

Malaysia has a total land area of 127,317 square miles (329,750 square kilometers). Peninsular Malaysia accounts for 40 percent of this land area. Between the peninsula and Borneo lies the South China Sea. The distance between the peninsula and East Malaysia at the closest point is about 400 miles (650 km).

Left: **Lush green vegetation covers the hills of the Cameron Highlands in Pahang. An *Orang Asli* (OH-rahng AS-lee) village sits on the hills.**

Peninsula Malaysia

In Peninsular Malaysia, a forested mountain range named Banjaran Titiwangsa runs 311 miles (500 km) from the Malaysian-Thai border in the north down to Negeri Sembilan in the south. Southern Malaysia has a relatively flat terrain and is the most developed region in the country. Many small islands surround the peninsula. These islands are very popular holiday destinations among locals and tourists alike. Many of these islands support beautiful coral reefs and diverse marine life.

East Malaysia

The landscape of East Malaysia is rather different from the peninsula because less economic development has taken place there. Many parts of East Malaysia still do not have paved roads and running water. East Malaysia is mountainous. The tallest mountain in Southeast Asia, Mount Kinabalu at 13,455 feet (4,101 meters), can be found in Kinabalu National Park, in the state of Sabah. Off the coast of Sabah lies Pulau Sipadan, a small island covered by rain forest. It is one of the top ten diving destinations in the world.

Above: Pulau Perhentian lies off the coast of Terengganu. The island is a popular site for diving, wind surfing, snorkeling, and swimming.

LEATHERBACK TURTLES

The leatherback turtle is one of the four species of giant turtles that nests on Malaysia's beaches.
(*A Closer Look, page 52*)

KINABALU NATIONAL PARK

The most prominent feature of Kinabalu National Park is Mount Kinabalu. The park is also prized for its hot springs and diverse flora and fauna.
(*A Closer Look, page 50*)

CAVES

Caves found in Malaysia are some of the largest and most spectacular limestone formations in the world.

(A Closer Look, page 44)

Left: Due to heavy rainfall, the soil in Malaysia's rain forests is usually thin and nutrient-poor. Many tropical trees have buttress roots to support their tall trunks in the thin soil. These roots also enable the trees to absorb nutrients from the decaying matter on the forest floor.

The Climate

Malaysia is a tropical country with a warm and humid climate all year round. The average temperature is 80° Fahrenheit (26.6° Celsius). The highlands, however, have cooler temperatures. The annual southwest monsoon blows from May to September and brings drier weather, while the northeast monsoon blows from November to March and brings heavy rain. The average rainfall is 100 inches (254 centimeters), with wide local variations.

Malaysia commonly experiences monsoon storms. Monsoon storms are heavy rainstorms accompanied by violent winds and a lot of thunder and lightning. These storms are heaviest during the northeast monsoon season. The areas that experience the highest rainfall during this season are the east coast of Peninsular Malaysia, the west coast of Sarawak, and the northeast coast of Sabah. The areas that lie further inland do not experience such heavy rainfall.

Below: The rhinoceros hornbill is easy to recognize because of its colorful bill and distinctive cackle.

Plants and Wildlife

Malaysia's landscape allows for the existence of many different animals and plants. The tropical lowland rain forests encourage the growth of thousands of species of flowering plants, ferns, palms, and trees. Many unique animal species are also found in these rain forests, including Sumatran rhinoceroses, tapirs, sambar deer, barking deer, tigers, leopards, macaques, gibbons, and orangutans.

National Parks

The increasing threat of deforestation has prompted the government to declare a large area of rain forest in the peninsula a national park. Located at the border of the states of Kelantan, Terengganu, and Pahang, the national park, Taman Negara, covers 1,677 square miles (4,343 square km). It is one of the oldest rain forests in the world. Malaysia has thirteen national parks: Two are found on the peninsula, and the rest are located on the island of Borneo.

Rajang River

Rajang River, the longest river in Malaysia, runs through Central Borneo. The river snakes about 350 miles (563 km) through the rain forest. It is the main source of water and primary mode of transportation for people living in the interior.

RAIN FORESTS

Some of Malaysia's most valuable treasures are its tropical rain forests.
(*A Closer Look, page 66*)

RAFFLESIA

One of the most amazing discoveries in the Malaysian rain forest is the rafflesia flower (*left*). Named after the founder of Singapore, Sir Thomas Stamford Raffles, the rafflesia is the world's largest flower. It can grow up to 39 inches (99 cm) in diameter. The full bloom lasts about five to seven days and gives off a foul smell to attract flies, which help pollinate the plant.

History

Early History

Malaysian history can be traced back only as far as the founding of the Malaccan empire, around A.D. 1400. Everything that happened before that is largely shrouded in legend. The only existing records of Malaysia's early history are some archaeological findings. Prehistoric tools, believed to be at least 34,000 years old, have been discovered in Perak and Kelantan, and some human remains, believed to date to 35,000–10,000 B.C., have been found in the Niah Caves in Sarawak.

The Malaccan Empire

The first important Malay kingdom in Southeast Asia was known as Srivijaya (now Palembang, Sumatra). When Srivijaya fell in the fourteenth century, the seat of power moved to Majapahit in Java. It was at this time that the Malaccan empire began to emerge. Fleeing the wrath of the Majapahit king, a Palembang prince, Parameswara, reached Melaka on the southwestern coast of Malaya. This prince is revered as the founder of Melaka. Under his rule, Melaka became an important trading port for Chinese, Malay, Indian, and Arab merchants. Parameswara converted from Hinduism to Islam, and Islam became the state religion.

THE PERANAKANS

The *Peranakans* (puh-RAH-nah-KAHNS) are the descendants of early Chinese immigrants who married indigenous Malays. This union has created a unique identity that combines the best of the two cultures.
(*A Closer Look, page 60*)

ORANG ASLI

The Orang Asli may have moved to Malaysia from Thailand or the Philippines. The indigenous people of Malaysia are believed to be their descendants.

Left: This is one of the limestone caves in Sarawak where some early human remains and cave paintings were discovered.

10

Left: The A' Famosa was a massive fortress built by the Portuguese to defend Melaka against attacks. Only a small portion of the fortress remains today.

MELAKA

Melaka's strategic location on the southwestern coast of Peninsular Malaysia made it a thriving trading center in the fourteenth century. Today, Melaka is a quiet seaside town with a rich cultural heritage.
(A Closer Look, page 56)

The Colonial Era

Attracted by the thriving trade in Melaka, the Portuguese conquered the state in 1511. During their rule, they tried to spread the Christian faith there. Only Christian traders were allowed to trade in Portuguese Melaka. This drove Indian and Arab traders, who were Hindus and Muslims, to other ports. As a result, trade in Melaka began to decline.

In 1641, the Dutch ousted the Portuguese to gain control of the spice trade. They did not redevelop the trading port in Melaka, and it continued to decline. Thus, the Malaccans hoped for improved conditions when the British took control from the Dutch at the end of the eighteenth century.

Under British Rule

The British had already established a colony in Pinang in 1786. They took control of Melaka in 1824 as part of the Anglo-Dutch treaty. The British set up their own system of public administration. They were also actively engaged in agriculture and tin mining. It was during this time that Chinese and Indian immigrants started to arrive in the area.

World War II and Beyond

In 1942, following the outbreak of World War II, the Japanese defeated the British in Malaya. The Malayan people initially welcomed the Japanese, who had promised to reclaim Asia from the colonial powers. When Japanese soldiers began to treat Malayans brutally, however, public opinion turned against the Japanese. When the war ended in 1945, the British returned to take power. They decided that Malaya should be allowed to self-govern, and they wanted to impose a plan known as the Malayan Union. Under this plan, the power of the Malay rulers would be reduced, and all citizens were to have equal rights regardless of their race. The union was opposed by the Malays, who saw it as a threat to their rights as the indigenous people of the country. In 1948, the Malay states formed the Federation of Malaya. Under the terms of the Federation, the sultans retained their power.

THE DEATH RAILWAY

The Japanese marched thousands of prisoners of war north to Thailand to build the infamous Death Railway. It was so named because of the massive numbers who died there as a result of dehydration and fatigue.

Left: Built by the British in 1818, St. George's Church in Penang is Malaysia's oldest Anglican church.

The Road to Independence

In their fight for independence, the Malays formed the United Malay National Organization (UMNO), the Chinese formed the Malaysian Chinese Association (MCA), and the Indians formed the Malaysian Indian Congress (MIC). These three parties then formed a coalition known as the Alliance. They lobbied for an election and won the election in 1955.

A new constitution was drawn up for Malaya, where the Malays were recognized as the indigenous people, and the government was to protect their political power and improve their economic status. In 1957, Malaya gained independence from the British. The first prime minister of Malaya was Tunku Abdul Rahman, the leader of the Alliance. In 1963, Singapore, Sabah, and Sarawak joined the Federation to form Malaysia. In 1965, Singapore withdrew from Malaysia. As an independent nation, Malaysia continued to retain the position that Malaya held as a member of the United Nations (U.N.) and Commonwealth of Nations. In 1967, it became one of the founding members of the Association of Southeast Asian Nations (ASEAN).

Above: On August 31, 1957, Tunku Abdul Rahman officiated a ceremony, declaring the independence of the Federation of Malaya from the British.

COMMONWEALTH OF NATIONS

The Commonwealth of Nations is a worldwide political organization of nations. The purpose of the Commonwealth is for consultation and cooperation. The British monarchy heads the Commonwealth.

Racial Riots

Some of the darkest moments in Malaysian history were the racial riots of 1969. During the 1960s, poverty was widespread among the Malays, while the Chinese and the Indians, by virtue of their trade as merchants, were wealthy. The races were further divided by linguistic differences and varied religious beliefs. After the riots ended, the government took active measures to promote social equality among the races. Government efforts included the implementation of the New Economic Policy (NEP) in the 1970s. The policy was designed to reduce poverty among the Malays.

A Developing Nation

Today, Malaysia is actively working to become a developed nation under the leadership of prime minister Dr. Mahathir bin Mohamad. Mahathir has initiated many policies that have helped improve the economic and social conditions of the country, including the introduction of heavy industries such as steel, cement, and automotive manufacturing.

Left: **Located in the Lake Gardens in Kuala Lumpur, the National Monument represents the nation's triumph over communism in the 1960s. The monument is the work of American sculptor Felix de Weldon.**

Tunku Abdul Rahman (1903–1990)

Revered as the father of independent Malaysia, Tunku Abdul Rahman helped found the UMNO in 1945 and was its president from 1952 to 1955. Within five years, he managed to unite the Malay, Chinese, and Indian communities, forming a coalition that won the first general election at a time when race relations were tense. He negotiated Malaya's independence from the British and gained it in 1957. He also conceived the idea of Malaysia and realized it in 1963. He was the country's first prime minister, a post he held from 1957 until he resigned in 1970, saddened by the race riots of May 13, 1969. Even after his resignation, he continued writing and giving speeches to promote national unity and religious tolerance.

Tunku Abdul Rahman

Chandra Muzaffar (1947–)

Chandra Muzaffar was dismissed as a professor from the Centre for Civilisational Dialogue at the University of Malaya in May 1999 because of his standing as a political activist. Many commentators view this as a politically motivated move. The Human Rights Watch Academic Freedom Committee wrote an appeal on his behalf to the Malaysian education minister, and it was endorsed by many universities in the United States. Chandra continues to be vice president of the National Justice Party and president of the International Movement for a Just World (JUST). He also sits on the board of directors for the International Movement Against All Forms of Discrimination and Racism (Belgium) and is a member of the Peace Council, a diverse committee of internationally renowned religious leaders working together for world peace.

Chandra Muzaffar

Marina Mahathir (1957–)

The eldest daughter of prime minister Dr. Mahathir bin Mohamad, Marina Mahathir is actively involved in promoting political and public awareness of issues relating to human immunodeficiency virus (HIV) and acquired immune deficiency syndrome (AIDS), both locally and abroad. She is president of the Malaysian AIDS Council (MAC) and a recipient of multiple awards, including the 1997 ASEAN Achievement Award for community service.

Marina Mahathir

Government and the Economy

Malaysia is a federation of thirteen states and three federal territories (Kuala Lumpur, Labuan, and Putrajaya) that are governed by a constitutional monarchy. The monarch holds office for a period of five years, after which the position rotates to other rulers of state, based on heredity. This paramount ruler, the *Yang Dipertuan Agong* (YANG dee-puh-TU-an ah-GUNG), is the nominal head of the federal government. This ruler is also the head of the military and the religious leader of the country. These positions are purely ceremonial, however, and the ruler does not participate in policy-making.

Under the constitution of 1957, political power lies with the Parliament. The Parliament consists of two chambers — the House of Representatives and the Senate. The leader of the party with the most seats in Parliament is appointed as the prime minister. The prime minister is the head of the cabinet and plays a crucial role in governing the country.

A FEDERATION OF STATES

As a federation, the states have the freedom to make their own laws in areas such as agriculture and customs. Sabah and Sarawak also have the freedom to make their own immigration laws.

PUTRAJAYA

To enable Malaysia to compete in the new information and technology economy, the "intelligent" city, Putrajaya, was developed. (*A Closer Look, page 64*)

Left: The Parliament House in Kuala Lumpur is home to the Senate and the House of Representatives.

Left: The State Secretariat Building in Johor Bahru was one of the last British colonial buildings to be constructed in the country. The Japanese used it as a fortress during World War II. Today, the building is home to various government offices.

KETUA KAMPONG AND TUAI RUMAH

Traditionally, the positions of the ketua kampong and tuai rumah were hereditary, but, today, the people in a village or longhouse elect their head based on their leadership qualities and their understanding of *adat* (ah-DUT) — the people's traditions and customary laws.

Local Administration

Smaller administrative units have been set up to assist the state governments in attending to the people's needs. These units exist mainly in the rural areas where communication between district members of Parliament and the people is difficult. The head of a village is the *ketua kampong* (kuh-TOO-ah kam-PUNG), and the head of a longhouse, the traditonal housing in East Malaysia, is the *tuai rumah* (too-AI roo-MAH). Cities have administration units, called municipal councils, in charge of waste disposal and the construction and maintenance of public areas and utilities.

KAPITAN

The Chinese community used to be governed by a *kapitan* (kah-pee-TAN). His duties were similar to the ketua kampong and tuai rumah. The most famous and powerful kapitan was Yap Ah Loy. He brought many Chinese to Malaysia.

Left: To start the latex flowing, a rubber tapper uses a sharp knife to shave a thin layer of bark off the rubber tree. The latex collects in the cup attached to the tree.

Agriculture

Between 1900 and 1950, when it was still under colonial rule, Malaysia's main export crop was rubber. The popularity of rubber as a crop fell, however, when prices hit an all-time low in the 1950s. Although oil palm was introduced to diversify Malaysia's agricultural products, another source of income was needed to further develop Malaysia's economy. It was in the early 1970s that the manufacturing industry was introduced. The first factories processed palm oil into cooking oil.

Manufacturing

By the early 1980s, Malaysia became the focal point of many foreign investors. Malaysia's government enticed these investors with special tax exemptions, cheap local labor, and industrial free zones, which were developed specifically for the purpose of building factories. These areas were equipped with highways and railways that ran to seaports. Goods manufactured within these industrial free zones could be exported with minimal customs documentation.

Today, many of Malaysia's top exports are products from the manufacturing industry, and include telecommunications and electronic equipment and parts. The United States is one of Malaysia's main trading partners.

RUBBER AND OIL PALM

Rubber trees and oil palms thrive in Malaysia, thanks to the country's vast expanse of land, suitable soil, and favorable weather.
(A Closer Look, page 68)

INDUSTRIAL FREE ZONES

The concept of industrial free zones has been so successful that Malaysia is now an advisor to many developing nations looking to implement this concept.

Cottage Industries

Cottage industries also play an important role in the Malaysian economy. Cottage industries are small-scale manufacturing industries that produce specialized items sold in the local market. This definition, however, is proving to be obsolete in Malaysia because many of the cottage industries are also involved in exporting their goods. The items produced by these industries include handicrafts, such as handwoven mats and baskets, *batik* (bah-TEEK) cloth, and woodcarvings, and local food products, such as soy sauce. This form of production still plays an important role in contributing to the income of families living in villages or rural areas.

Heavy Industries

Since the early 1990s, Malaysia has also been involved in heavy industries, including the automotive and steel industries. The Malaysian automotive industry has proved to be very successful. There are currently two Malaysian-made car brands — Proton and Perodua. In a survey conducted by the United Kingdom Consumer's Association, Proton was ranked as one of the "Top 10 Most Reliable Cars in the U.K."

PROTON

The Proton car company was incorporated in 1983, and, today, it is Malaysia's leading car manufacturer, with the capability to produce a car from concept to manufacture.

Left: A newly assembled Proton car is inspected at the Proton factory in Shah Alam, Selangor.

People and Lifestyle

Ethnic Diversity

Malaysia is a melting pot of many ethnic groups. Much of this diversity arose because of Malaysia's ideal location at the center of major trading routes. Malaysians can be classified as *bumiputera* (boo-mih-poo-TRAH) and non-bumiputera. Bumiputera is a collective term used to refer to people of ethnic Malay origin and includes the Orang Asli. The bumiputera account for 58 percent of Malaysia's population. The non-bumiputera consists mainly of people of other ethnicities, including Chinese (27 percent) and Indians (8 percent). The other 7 percent of the population is made up of various ethnic groups including Eurasians.

The distinction between the bumiputera and non-bumiputera came about in the 1970s, when the government introduced the NEP (New Economic Policy) to improve the status of the Malays. By introducing the NEP, the government managed to lower the poverty level and raise the rate of literacy of this lower income group.

INDIGENOUS PEOPLE

Malaysia's indigenous people are an important component of the country's rich heritage. Each ethnic group has its own language, beliefs, and culture.
(A Closer Look, page 49)

Below: **The people of Malaysia are a harmonious blend of many cultures and ethnic groups.**

Left: These Malay women trade fresh produce and cooked food at a local market in Sabah.

LONGHOUSE LIVING

In Sarawak, small groups of tribal people continue to make the traditional longhouse their home.
(A Closer Look, page 54)

Poverty

At present, an estimated 5 percent of the population still lives in poverty. East Malaysia has a higher proportion of poor people than the peninsula due to the lower level of development in the East Malaysian states. While the government is working to improve the standard of living in East Malaysia, much remains to be done.

People of East Malaysia

Numerous indigenous groups reside in the forests and coastal areas of East Malaysia. Some of these groups continue to practice their traditional customs, live in communal dwellings, and survive by farming, hunting, and fishing. Within Sabah, there are thirty-one different indigenous groups. They include the Kadazan and Bajau. Sarawak is home to twenty-six indigenous groups, including the Iban, Bidayuh, and Penan.

NOMADIC TRIBESMEN

A small group of Penans still lead a nomadic existence in Sarawak. They are one of the last surviving nomadic tribes in the world.

21

Family

The Malaysian family is generally close-knit. Three or four generations may live under the same roof. In rare cases, five generations live in one household. Large families were common in the past because people married at a young age and had children soon after. Family members live in harmony and the young are taught to respect their elders. The older generation is also looked to for advice and guidance.

With the exception of the Minangkabau people who migrated from the Indonesian island of Sumatra and now reside in Negeri Sembilan, the Malaysian society is generally patriarchal.

The roles of husband and wife are largely conventional. Men are usually the sole breadwinners and providers, while women are usually homemakers who manage the financial transactions related to the family. These traditional roles, however, are slowly changing. With an increase in literacy levels and the growing number of females entering higher education, more women are now entering into the professional workforce.

MINANGKABAU SOCIETY

The Minangkabau are traditionally matriarchal. The women are the dominant party and the head of the household.

Left: **A Malay family goes on an outing on a motorcycle in Kedah.**

Left: Three young siblings sit on the concrete steps outside their home in Kuala Kangsar.

Children

Malaysian families vary in size. Parents in rural areas may have five or more children. In the larger towns and cities, however, people may choose to have only one or two children. This is due to changing preferences as well as the higher cost of living in urban areas.

Children are taught to respect their elders, but this does not mean that they cannot speak their minds. In fact, children are encouraged to express themselves respectfully to their elders, without losing their temper or throwing a tantrum.

Divorce

As a society that is largely inclined toward Islam and Buddhism, marriage and the family unit are considered sacred in Malaysia. Divorce was almost nonexistent until the late 1980s. All divorce procedures have to be taken to the *Syariah* (SHAH-ree-ah) courts. The Syariah courts handle all legal issues related to marriage and the family.

I DIVORCE YOU

Islamic law dictates that for a man to divorce his wife, he must first declare "I divorce you" three times in a courthouse before his wife and a judge.

Primary Education

The public education system in Malaysia includes preschool, primary, secondary, and post-secondary education. Children can go to preschool for up to three years, beginning at age four or five. Children enter primary school at age six or seven. Most schools instruct classes in the *Bahasa Melayu* (bah-HAA-sah MUH-lah-yoo), or Malay language, but other schools teach using Chinese, English, or Tamil. Students in these schools also receive Malay- and English-language instruction.

Secondary and Pre-University Education

For most students, secondary school begins at age thirteen. Secondary education is divided into three levels — lower secondary, middle secondary, and pre-university. The language used for all instruction in Malaysia's secondary schools is Malay. Compulsory subjects include mathematics, art, science, history, geography, English, and Islamic religious and moral studies. Foreign languages, industrial arts, home science, commerce, economics, agriculture, Chinese, and Tamil are offered electives. Students must pass an exam to advance from lower to middle education. At the middle secondary level, students take another exam to determine whether they will continue to the pre-university level or enter vocational training.

THE MADRASAH

Some parents choose to send their children to a *madrasah* (mah-DRAH-sah) — a private Islam school — instead of enrolling them in the national school system.

Left: Computers are becoming common in Malaysian classrooms.

Universities

Malaysia has many local universities throughout the country that offer degrees and diplomas in various fields of study. The main language of instruction at these universities is Bahasa Melayu. As such, these universities present a major challenge for foreign students who do not know the language.

The Universiti Telekom (Unitele) in Malaysia was renamed Multimedia University (MMU) in 1997. It has two campuses, one in Cyberjaya and one in Melaka. One of the main roles of this multimedia university is to support the government's move toward making Malaysia an information technology hub for the region.

Vocational and Private Colleges

Vocational schools and private colleges provide alternatives to the standard education path. Vocational schools teach technical subjects, including construction, electrical and electronic circuitry, and engine repair.

Private colleges offer a wide range of courses, from highly advanced programs to degree courses in business management and accounting. Private colleges usually run degree courses with the assistance of a foreign university. The overseas university awards the degree. The disadvantage of this system is its high cost. In most cases, only people from the upper middle class can afford to attend this type of college.

Religion

Although the official religion of Malaysia is Islam, the constitution provides for religious freedom in the country. Malaysia's ethnic diversity influences the religious inclinations of the people. The Malay people are predominantly Muslim, the Chinese are Buddhist or Taoist, and the Indians are either Hindus or Sikhs. Christianity is also practiced by some Chinese, Indians, and Eurasians. In East Malaysia, some indigenous people practice shamanism and many others are Christian.

Above: **This Muslim man meditates in the serenity of a mosque in Kuala Kangsar, Perak.**

Islam

Muslims do not eat pork or drink alcohol. They are required to pray five times a day: just before 6 A.M., at noon, 4 P.M., dusk, and after dark. All major buildings and institutions in Malaysia are equipped with a public prayer room called a *surau* (soo-RAU). Muslims can go to the surau to pray at these designated times. Every Friday, Muslims gather at a local mosque for an hour-long prayer session that begins at 12:30 P.M.

PRAYING TOWARD MECCA

When they pray, Muslims always face toward Mecca in Saudi Arabia. Mecca is the birthplace of the prophet Muhammad, the founder of Islam.

Left: **The Ubudiah Mosque in Kuala Kangsar, Perak, is regarded by many as the most beautiful mosque in Malaysia.**

Other Religions

The main pillar of the Buddhist faith is the law of cause and effect. Buddhists believe that a person's good or evil deeds eventually result in reward or punishment. In Malaysia, Buddhism bears the influence of Taoism and Confucianism.

The Hindus believe in reincarnation based on a person's deeds in life. Doing good deeds and suppressing evil will enable a Hindu to be reincarnated into a higher being. The process of reincarnation continues until the soul attains a unity with God.

Christianity was introduced into Malaysia during the colonial era. Traces of this influence can still be seen in churches left behind in Melaka by the Portuguese and Dutch, and in George Town, Penang, by the British. Some of the indigenous people in East Malaysia are also Christians.

Language and Literature

A Multilingual Society

The official language of Malaysia is Bahasa Melayu, but many other languages are also widely used within the country. These languages came to Malaysia with immigrants from various countries.

Local Dialects

Mandarin is commonly spoken by the Chinese, who also use dialects such as Cantonese, Hakka, Teochew, and Hokkien. When people from different dialect groups need to speak to each other, they use Mandarin. Many Indian dialects are also spoken in Malaysia. These include Malayalam, Telugu, and Hindi. The most popular Indian language used is Tamil because the majority of the Indians living in Malaysia are Tamils.

Today, the language of instruction in most schools is Malay. Students may choose to learn Chinese or Tamil while all students are taught English. Local newspapers are available in Malay, English, Chinese, and Tamil.

Left: **These primary school students are taking part in a poetry recital competition.**

Malay Annals

One of the most important Malaysian texts is the *Malay Annals* or *Sejarah Melayu*, written by Tun Sri Lanang. This historian lived in Melaka during the peak of the Malaccan empire. This book was the first written account of the history of the Malay Archipelago. It records the lifestyle of the early Malay royalty and is used as a historical resource for students and scholars alike.

Malaysian Literature

During the nationalist movement of the 1940s, stories were written that called for the unification of the races against the colonial rulers. When independence was achieved, these writers started writing on the themes of friendship, unity, patriotism, and love. One of the few living legends of this post-independence era is A. Samad Said (1935–), who began his career as a journalist and moved on to write poetry, short stories, plays, and novels. His mastery of these different genre won him the title of National Literary Figure in 1985. He also won the Southeast Asia Write Award in 1979. His most famous work is a novel entitled *Salina* (1965). The novel depicts the mindset of the Malaysians after facing hardship under Japanese rule.

POETRY

Pantun (pahn-TUHN) is the most basic form of Malay poetry. It reflects the diplomacy and gentle nature of the Malays. The meanings are always implied and take the form of suggestions. The *syair* (sha-IR) tells a story and is usually accompanied by traditional Malay music. The *sajak* (sah-JAK) is a form of modern Malay free verse. It is very dramatic and read like a song.

Arts

Malaysian art is highly influenced by religion and culture. Indian and Chinese art forms can be traced back to their countries of origin. Indian dances were performed in devotion to the Hindu gods, and colorful sculptures were made to adorn temples. Chinese dances originated as court dances, while Chinese paintings and sculptures were motivated by nature and Chinese beliefs. In the same way, Islam had a great influence on Malay art. Its motifs and themes are incorporated into Malay dances, crafts, paintings, and architecture. Royal patronage for these art forms allowed them to flourish, and they continue today as Malay art.

Opposite: **An Iban woman weaves traditional Iban clothing in the Kuching Cultural Village in Sarawak.**

Below: **The traditional art of batik is demonstrated at the Central Market in Kuala Lumpur.**

Visual Art

Malaysian visual art includes traditional crafts, such as weaving, batik, woodcarving, pewter and sliver work. In weaving, the leaves of the *pandan* (pahn-DAHN), *mengkuang* (meng-KOO-ang), rattan, bamboo, and *bertam* (ber-TUM) are used. Woven products include mats, baskets, and other household items.

In batik printing, patterns are drawn onto cloth using liquid wax. Once the wax dries, the cloth is dyed. The area with wax is shielded from the dye. The wax is then removed from the cloth by dipping it in boiling water. This process is repeated several times until the pattern is complete.

WAYANG KULIT

Wayang kulit (WAH-yang koo-LIT) is a traditional art form. It takes great skill to create the puppets and manipulate them during a performance.
(*A Closer Look, page 72*)

Dance

Malay dances can generally be divided into ancient or court dances, theatrical dances, and modern dance. The ancient dances once performed in the Malay courts and accompanied by ancient musical instruments are no longer popular today.

Today, one of the most popular forms of theatrical dance is the *mak yong* (MAK yong). Originating from Kelantan, the mak yong is a mix of ballet, opera, romantic drama, and comedy. It is accompanied by an orchestra of drums, gongs, and violins. The mak yong is different from modern western theater in that no props are used, and a woman usually plays the male lead role. A performance is also never completed in one night. It usually stretches over five nights.

The *zapin* (zah-PEEN) is a modern Malay dance. It is usually performed at cultural events held locally or abroad. This dance portrays the gentleness of the Malay people. The dance was originally performed by male dancers, but, today, female dancers also play an important role.

In East Malaysia, each ethnic group has its own dance forms. The dances imitate the movements of animals and retell tribal legends and folklore. An example is the *ngajat* (naa-JAT), a dance of the Iban.

Above: **Most Malay dances involve the various movements of sitting, kneeling, and standing, as well as hand gestures.**

Architecture

Malaysian architecture combines colonial influence and Islamic heritage. Examples of Dutch and Portuguese styles include the Stadthuys, A'Famosa, St. Paul's Church, and Christ Church in Melaka. Modern buildings boast a unique Malaysian style that combines modern lines with Islamic motifs. One such example is the Dayabumi Complex in Kuala Lumpur. The complex's high-vaulted arches are reminiscent of those found in mosques.

Malaysia's modern architecture also draws inspiration from the traditional dwellings of ethnic groups such as the Minangkabau. The distinctive horn-shaped roof at the entrance of the Maybank building in Kuala Lumpur is modeled after the roofs of Minangkabau architecture.

THE PETRONAS TOWERS

By virtue of its spires, the Petronas Towers have surpassed the Sears Tower in Chicago as the world's tallest building. (*A Closer Look, page 63*)

In the older towns and cities, such as Melaka and George Town, many old shophouses line the streets. These two-story shophouses were mostly built in the early twentieth century. They allowed the merchants to live and conduct their business on the same premise.

Houses built on stilts are a distinctive feature of Malaysian architecture. These houses were designed to keep the occupants cool in the humid tropical weather and dry in the event of floods. Such houses can still be found in rural areas in Malaysia.

Above: The Perak Royal Museum used to be the Istana Kenangan — the former palace of the sultan of Perak. It was built without any nails, and it has woven bamboo walls.

33

Leisure and Festivals

Malaysians love having fun and enjoy both traditional and modern pastimes. Traditional pastimes that are still pursued today include kite flying, top spinning, and playing *congkak* (CHONG-kak). In larger towns and cities, people also enjoy modern pastimes such as going to the movies.

Kite Flying

Traditional Malaysian kites can extend up to 12 feet (3.66 m) and require a lot of strength and stamina to control. The most famous type of Malaysian kite is the *wau bulan* (WOW BOO-lan), or moon kite, named for its crescent-shaped tail. Kite-flying tournaments are very popular in Malaysia. The most famous tournament is held in Kelantan. It draws both local and foreign contestants with multicolored kites of different shapes and sizes. Winners are judged on the kite's design and how high the kite can fly.

P. RAMLEE

The multitalented P. Ramlee was a famous Malaysian artiste in the 1950s. Watching the movies in which he starred or directed was a popular pastime.
(A Closer Look, page 58)

Below: **The colorful wau bulan originated in Kelantan. The patterns on the kite are usually of local flora and fauna.**

Top Spinning

Top, or *gasing* (GAH-sing), spinning is particularly popular in Kelantan and Terengganu. Top spinning tournaments are held annually and players from all over the world come to take part in these tournaments. This sport is not child's play since the top weighs about 11 pounds (5 kilograms). Throwing this top requires strength, coordination, and expertise. The top is first thrown onto an elevated platform and then transferred to the flattened end of a stick where it is left to spin. An expert top spinner can leave his or her top spinning for up to two hours! The winner of the tournament is the person who throws the longest-spinning top.

Congkak

Women often enjoy playing indoor games. One such game is congkak, a two-player game of patience, strategy, and mental calculation. It is played using a boat-shaped block of wood with a hole at either end and five to nine smaller holes on each side. Depending on the number of holes on the board, each of the holes is filled with five to nine counters. Game counters are usually shells, stones, seeds, or marbles. Players sit facing each other and compete to collect counters, placing them in the larger hole on their right. This is known as their storehouse. The player who manages to collect the most counters wins the game.

Sports

Malaysians love sports such as soccer, badminton, and *sepak takraw* (seh-PAHK TAHK-raw) because these sports do not require expensive equipment or a formal setting in order to play. Malaysians can be seen enjoying these sports in open fields, school courtyards, and even driveways of residential estates.

Soccer

Malaysians take soccer very seriously and faithfully support their favorite teams. Soccer is played both in rural areas and big cities. People often spend hours debating a game they saw on television. The most popular international league in Malaysia is the English Premier League.

Malaysia has two soccer leagues of its own. The first league is played by teams from the thirteen states of Malaysia, and the second league is played by teams from various government institutions, such as the armed forces. Each league has a total of twelve teams. The top eight teams from the first league and the top five teams from the second league go on to play for the Malaysian Cup. All the football leagues in Malaysia are governed by the Football Association of Malaya (FAM).

SEPAK TAKRAW

Sepak takraw has been described as volleyball, gymnastics, and soccer rolled into one sport. Sepak takraw is enjoyed because of its fast pace and athletic demands.
(A Closer Look, page 70)

Left: **These Malay schoolboys are having a friendly soccer match in Pulau Pangkor.**

Left: **Alex Yoong is Malaysia's first F1 driver. He made his debut in the Italian Grand Prix in 2001.**

Badminton

Badminton experienced an increase in popularity in Malaysia when the nation won the Thomas Cup in 1992. The Thomas Cup is the most coveted trophy in the badminton world. Today, badminton is a sport enjoyed both by adults and children.

Motor Sports

Malaysians also enjoy car and motorcycle racing. The country has three major racing circuits. The biggest development in Malaysian motor sports was the construction of the Sepang Formula One (F1) Circuit just outside Kuala Lumpur. International racing organizations and drivers acknowledge that the Sepang F1 Circuit is one of the best tracks in the world. Costing approximately MYR 456 million (U.S. $120 million), this track was built according to the specifications of the Fédération Internationale de l'Automobile (FIA). Since opening in December 1998, the Sepang F1 Circuit has become one of the venues for annual F1 events.

Festivals

As a multicultural country, Malaysia observes many festivals and holidays throughout the year. The nation has approximately thirty public holidays each year. Many of these holidays are religious or cultural festivals. Out of respect for other races and cultures, many Malaysians observe the festivals of ethnic groups other than their own. For example, during the Muslim *Hari Raya Aidilfitri* (HAH-ree RYE-ah ih-dih-FIT-rih) celebrations, Chinese and Indians usually visit the homes of their Muslim friends and share in their joy. Similarly, during the Chinese New Year festivities, non-Chinese people are invited to the homes of their Chinese friends, and they are treated to a feast of Chinese New Year sweets and tidbits.

Muslim Festivals

The biggest celebration of the Islamic faith is Hari Raya Aidilfitri. This holiday is celebrated after a month-long fasting period called Ramadan. Another Muslim event that is celebrated with much fanfare is *Hari Raya Haji* (HAH-ree RYE-ah HAH-jee), which marks the beginning of the pilgrimage season. Muslims are required by their religion to perform a pilgrimage to the holy shrine of Mecca, if their finances permit.

HARI RAYA AIDILFITRI

Hari Raya Aidilfitri is a joyous occasion for Muslims as families gather for meals and to exchange blessings.
(A Closer Look, page 46)

Left: A Hindu family offers prayers to the deities in celebration of Deepavali.

Chinese Festivals

Malaysian Chinese celebrate their new year in a noisy way. This is not a religious festival but a cultural one. The Chinese prepare for the festival by cleaning and decorating their homes. On the eve of the new year, the extended family gathers together for a reunion dinner. Fireworks light up the sky at midnight. Although the official holiday lasts only three days, the festivities carry on until the fifteenth day, or *chap goh mei* (CHAP goh meh). On this day, families cook special dinners and light lanterns outside their homes. Many towns with predominantly Chinese populations celebrate with parades organized by different Chinese associations.

Hindu Festivals

The Hindus celebrate *Deepavali* (dee-PAH-vah-lee), the festival of lights. According to Hindu mythology, it was on this day that the god Vishnu defeated a demon that had kept the world in darkness. When the demon was destroyed, light was restored. The Hindus celebrate this triumph by illuminating their homes with light and oil lamps. On Deepavali, the family wakes up early to pray and have an elaborate breakfast together. Visitors usually arrive in the late morning and stay for lunch. This practice of eating and entertaining continues over the following two days.

HARVEST FESTIVAL

Indigenous groups in East Malaysia celebrate the harvest festival. During this festival, the people brew their own wine from sticky rice and offer it to guests. The wine is usually served in huge cups made of bamboo. They greet their guests by performing traditional dances and serving traditional food. These foods include different kinds of meat and rice cooked in bamboo.

Food

Food is an important part of Malaysian culture. Most festivals and functions are celebrated with large feasts. Malaysia's diverse cultural makeup also contributes to an exciting dining experience. Apart from restaurants, there are hawker stalls that sell Chinese, Malay, and Indian food.

The tolerance and respect Malaysians have for each other's cultures can be seen in their wide culinary tastes. A number of dishes unique to various ethnic groups are now known as Malaysian dishes. This includes *roti canai* (ROH-tee CHA-nai), a flat Indian pancake eaten with curry, and *nasi lemak* (NAH-see ler-MAHK), a Malay dish of rice cooked in coconut milk.

Malay Cuisine

Malay cooking involves the use of large amounts of herbs and spices to create spicy dishes, which are always full of flavor. Beef, mutton, chicken, and fish are popular meat choices for Malay dishes, which are usually served with rice. Most of these dishes come with a rich gravy, thickened with fresh coconut milk. Some popular dishes are *ayam goreng* (AH-yum GO-rehng), a rice dish served with deep fried chicken flavored with tumeric and curry powder, and *satay* (SAH-tay), a dish of marinated meat skewered and cooked over a charcoal fire and served with a peanut sauce.

Above: **Street dining is common throughout Malaysia. This stall is in Kuala Lumpur.**

RICE

Rice is a staple food among Malaysians. It is eaten for breakfast, lunch, and dinner.

HALAL FOOD

Muslims may consume only halal certified food and drinks. This means that the food must be prepared without pork or lard. Restaurants and stalls serving halal food indicate this with a halal certification label.

Left: **A Chinese hawker fries banana fritters in a wok in Ipoh.**

Chinese Cuisine

In Chinese cooking, vegetable and meat dishes are usually prepared by steaming or stir-frying in oil that has first been made fragrant with chopped garlic. These dishes are served with rice or porridge. Noodles are also eaten as an alternative to rice. Noodles are either stir-fried, served in clear soup, or flavored with a small amount of sauce. The most common noodle dishes are fishball or wonton noodles, egg noodles with fishballs or wontons, and *char kway teow* (CHAH kway tee-ow), flat noodles that are stir-fried in black sauce.

Fruits

Many tropical fruits grow in Malaysia. They include thirst-quenching and refreshing varieties, such as rambutans, watermelons, star fruits, pineapples, and pomelos. The durian, which is a spiky, pungent fruit with a soft, creamy, yellow flesh, is a favorite fruit among Malaysians. Most of these fruits are seasonal, but imported fruits, such as apples, pears, and oranges, are available all year round.

FAST FOOD

A phenomenon that is rapidly catching on in Malaysia is fast food. American fast-food chains, such as Burger King and McDonald's, are becoming commonplace in cities and towns. Although fast food costs more than hawker food, meeting and eating at fast food restaurants is a growing trend among young Malaysians.

41

A CLOSER LOOK AT MALAYSIA

Since gaining independence, Malaysia has become one of the fastest-developing countries in the world. As Malaysians pursue the status of developed nation, the country continues to maintain its traditional practices and culture. This makes the country an interesting blend of old and new. In cities, modern shopping malls nestle between old shophouses, selling traditional items such as Chinese herbal medicines and wooden clogs. Air-conditioned western restaurants sit next to makeshift food stalls. Business executives in western suits jostle with people in traditional dress.

Opposite: **Kuala Lumpur is Malaysia's most cosmopolitan city.**

Under prime minister Dr. Mahathir bin Mohamad, Malaysia is working toward fulfilling Vision 2020. This is a set of objectives that the government has designed to turn Malaysia into a fully industrialized country by the year 2020. Besides economic development, the government is also working toward shaping Malaysia politically, socially, spiritually, psychologically, and culturally through Vision 2020. The ultimate goal of this vision is to make Malaysia a country that is socially cohesive and progressive, with an economy that is competitive and dynamic, in order to meet future challenges.

Above: **Local fishing boats line the Dasar Sabak Beach in Kelantan. This beach was where Japanese troops first landed in 1941, before their invasion of the peninsula during World War II.**

Caves

Some of the world's most beautiful caves are found in Malaysia. Most of these caves are limestone formations. The Batu Caves in Selangor are the most famous cave network in the peninsula. Three major caves can be found in this network: Temple Cave, Dark Cave, and Gallery Cave. Temple Cave is the most visited cave. It houses statues of Hindu deities, and thousands of Hindu devotees flock to this cave during *Thaipusam* (TIE-poo-sahm). The cave sits on a hill, and the only way up is by climbing 272 steps!

Dark Cave is virtually untouched and hosts a large number of cave-dwelling fauna, some of which are unique to Malaysia. To visit the cave, permission has to be obtained from the Malaysian Nature Society. Gallery Cave lies behind Dark Cave and is home to many statues and paintings depicting Hindu mythology.

In East Malaysia, two of the better-known cave networks are the Mulu Caves and the Niah Caves. The Mulu Caves are located in the Gunung Mulu National Park in Sarawak. This network houses the world's largest natural chamber, the Sarawak Chamber, and the world's largest cave passage, Deer Cave. Although less impressive than the Mulu Caves, the Niah Caves are an important archaeological site. In these caves, archaeologists have found evidence of human settlements dating back 40,000 years. Lying near the Niah Caves are Great Cave and Painted

Above: **A Hindu devotee bearing a *kavadi* (KAH-vah-dee) makes his way up to Temple Cave.**

THAIPUSAM

Thaipusam is the celebration of the birthday of Lord Muruga. A main feature of the festival is the carrying of the kavadi as an act of penitence. A kavadi is a semicircular frame decorated with colorful tinsel, peacock feathers, and flowers. It sits on the devotee's shoulders and is secured by piercing metal hooks and skewers through the devotee's cheeks, tongue, and skin.

Left: **The entrance to Deer Cave is over 328 feet (100 m) high.**

Cave. It was in Great Cave that an early human skull and ancient tools and ornaments were discovered. Painted Cave is home to a number of prehistoric wall paintings. The discovery of boat-shaped coffins in this cave has led archaeologists to conclude that it was an early burial chamber. The Niah Caves are also an important source of bat droppings, which is used as fertilizer.

Hari Raya Aidilfitri

Hari Raya Aidilfitri is also known as *Hari Raya Puasa* (HAH-ree RYE-ah PWAH-sah). *Hari Raya* means "a great day" and *Puasa* comes from a Sanskrit word meaning "fasting" or "abstinence." While there is no direct translation for the word *Aidilfitri*, *fitri* refers to the giving of alms to the poor. Thus, Hari Raya Aidilfitri, or Hari Raya Puasa, marks the end of a period of fasting and is a reminder of the need to practice charity.

The month-long fasting period, Ramadan, is observed during the ninth month of the Muslim calendar. During this period, the Muslims are required to fast from dawn to dusk. They wake before sunrise and have breakfast after their morning prayers. After that, they are not allowed to eat, drink, or smoke until sunset, when the family and perhaps some very close friends will gather to break their fast.

Ramadan is a time of inward reflection for Muslims as they abstain from food and drink and maintain discipline in their thoughts and deeds. By fasting, Muslims are also able to experience the pain and suffering of the poor and hungry.

Left: **During Hari Raya Aidilfitri, it is customary for the younger members of the family to seek forgiveness from their elders.**

As an act of faith, Muslims are required to make compulsory payment. This payment is called *zakat* (ZAH-kaht). In Malaysia, it is usually collected as taxes. The amount of money people are required to give depends on their income. The money collected is then distributed to the poor to enable them to enjoy Hari Raya Aidilfitri, too.

Hari Raya Aidilfitri is celebrated on the first day of *Syawal* (SYE-waw), the tenth month of the Muslim lunar calendar. To prepare for the festivities, Muslims clean and decorate their homes and purchase or bake cookies and cakes.

In Malaysia, Hari Raya Aidilfitri is observed with two national holidays, but the celebrations usually last for a week. On the day of the festival, Muslims rise early and put on their new *baju Melayu* (BAH-joo MUH-lah-yoo). The younger members of the family then greet their elders and seek their forgiveness for any wrongs committed over the year. After breakfast, the family proceeds to the mosque for prayers. Family members may also visit the graves of departed loved ones. Throughout the rest of the celebrations, family and friends visit one another.

People of other races and religions also visit their Muslim friends during Hari Raya. They are usually served a wide variety of Malay specialties, including *ketupat* (KUH-too-paht), a rice cake cooked in woven palm leaves, and *rendang* (RUHNG-dahng), a rich and spicy meat curry.

Indigenous People

The indigenous people, or Orang Asli, are the oldest inhabitants of Malaysia. More than sixty ethnic groups are recognized as bumiputeras, and each group has its own language and culture. The languages of the Orang Asli are known collectively as *Aslian* (AS-lee-an) languages.

The Orang Asli live in the rain forests or near the coastal areas. The groups living in the rain forests may practice crop cultivation, hunting, and gathering. The groups living along the coasts are usually fishers. The Orang Asli are very resourceful. They build houses using dry leaves and twigs. These shelters are strong enough to withstand tropical storms.

In the eighteenth and nineteenth centuries, Orang Asli villages were commonly raided, and women and children were captured to be sold as slaves. This changed through the efforts of H.D. Noone, the director of the Perak Museum in the 1930s. He fought to preserve the rights of the Orang Asli. He also proposed the idea of patterned settlements, where the Orang Asli could develop their agricultural skills and practice their own handicraft.

The Orang Asli in East Malaysia are fascinating because of their virtually undisturbed culture. Twenty-six ethnic groups live in Sarawak, each still practicing its own culture and speaking its own language. The most well-known ethnic group is the Iban. Once fearsome warriors and headhunters, the Iban are peaceful people today. Visitors to the Iban villages are treated with utmost respect and hospitality.

The Penan are renowned as the only nomadic group still existing in Sarawak today. They are hunter-gatherers, and they live deep in the rain forest. They hunt with blowpipes and gather wild fruit, roots, and plants. They are also skilled in weaving baskets, mats, and other household items. The Penan also specialize in making a long knife known as the parang.

The largest ethnic group in Sabah is the Kadazan, who make up a third of the population of Sabah. The Bajau are also a well-known ethnic group that can be classified into two clans: the peaceful east coast Bajau, skilled boat-builders and fishers who live mainly on their boats; and the more aggressive west coast Bajau, skilled horseriders who also rear cattle.

Above: **The Orang Asli weave household items that are sold at the local market. This mother is weaving a hat, while her son sits quietly by her side.**

Opposite: **An Orang Asli man hunts with his blowpipe. The blowpipe is made of bamboo and can be accurate within a range of 66 feet (20 m).**

Kinabalu National Park

Lying approximately 56 miles (90 km) west of the capital city of Kota Kinabalu, the Kinabalu National Park is one of the major attractions of Sabah. The park spans 288 square miles (746 square km) and officially became a national park in 1964.

Mount Kinabalu

The most imposing feature of the national park is the majestic 13,455-foot (4,101-m) high Mount Kinabalu. The highest mountain in Southeast Asia, Mount Kinabalu is still growing at a rate of 0.2 inches (5 millimeters) per year. The awesome height and jagged peaks of Mount Kinabalu were revered by the indigenous Kadazan people, who regarded it as their spirit homeland and a resting place for their dead. The name *Kinabalu* is derived from the Kadazan term *Akinabalu,* meaning "revered place of the dead." Despite its height, Mount Kinabalu is relatively easy to climb because climbers do not need special skills

Below: **Visitors to the park enjoy trekking up the gentle incline of Mount Kinabalu.**

or climbing equipment. As such, each year, the park attracts thousands of visitors eager to scale the mountain. The climb up the mountain takes approximately two to three days.

Poring Hot Springs

Apart from Mount Kinabalu, another attraction of the Kinabalu National Park is the hot springs. These springs were first used by the Japanese during World War II and are now known as the Poring Hot Springs. The springs have been piped into several Japanese-style baths. The sulfur content in the water is believed to be beneficial for various skin ailments.

A Historical Site

Besides its natural heritage, Kinabalu National Park is also part of the historical site of the Sandakan-Ranau death march. Sandakan is a small town on the eastern coast of Sabah, and Ranau lies in the foothills of Mount Kinabalu. In January 1945, during World War II, Japanese soldiers made about 2,400 Australian and British prisoners of war march from Sandakan to Ranau. The distance between the two towns is approximately 149 miles (240 km). Of those 2,400 soldiers, only six escaped and survived.

A THRIVING HABITAT

The varying altitudes within the park have contributed to the richness of its flora and fauna. The giant rafflesia flower, the world's largest pitcher plant, and more than one thousand species of orchid can be found here.

51

Leatherback Turtles

The leatherback turtle (*Dermochelys coriacea*) is the largest species of sea turtle in the world. Its distinctive features and abilities, compared to other turtles, have granted it its own taxonomic family, *Dermochelys*. Although leatherbacks hatch in the tropics, they are known to forage in very cold waters. They can also dive deep into the sea. The main diet of the leatherback turtle is jellyfish and seaweed.

Adult leatherback turtles range in size from 4 to 8 feet (1.2 to 2.4 m). They can weigh between 700 and 2,000 pounds (318 and 907 kg). They are named for the leathery shell, or carapace, that covers their body. The carapace is slightly flexible and because it does not form any right angles with the underbelly, the leatherback turtle is more rounded in shaped than other turtles. Another distinctive feature of leatherbacks are the seven ridges that run lengthwise across their carapace. Their skin is black and speckled with gray, white, and pink blotches.

Below: **The Rantau Abang Beach is one of only six places in the world visited by the nesting leatherback turtle. A turtle hatchery has been set up here in an effort to halt the declining numbers of leatherback turtles.**

Left: Turtle eggs have soft shells and are about the size of billiard balls.

The leatherback turtles favor open, sandy beaches, such as those in Terengganu, for nesting. They can lay between 60 to 120 eggs per nest and may nest four to five times per season. They dig holes as deep as 3 feet (0.9 m) to lay their eggs. The eggs take about sixty days to hatch. The hatchlings are about 2.4 inches (6 cm) long and weigh just a few ounces (grams). Many do not hatch because the eggs are vulnerable to predators that dig them up from the nest. Those that hatch need to crawl to the sea. They cannot stay too long away from the sea or they will dehydrate and die. In the sea, the hatchlings and young turtles may also be eaten by fish or killed by boat propellers and pollution. The leatherback turtle was classified as an endangered species in 1970.

While the leatherback turtles once populated Rantau Abang beach in Terengganu, the numbers have declined drastically. The leatherbacks are exploited as tourist attractions, affecting their inclination to nest. The eggs are believed to have medicinal values and are harvested for consumption. Adult leatherbacks also face the danger of being caught and killed in fishing nets. A study by the Sea Turtle Research Unit at the University College of Science and Technology Malaysia estimated that fishing nets have the potential to kill some 400 leatherbacks each year. Conservation activities and state regulations have been drawn up to protect the leatherbacks, but marine pollution and fishing activities continue to threaten their survival.

TURTLE TEARS

It has been said that sea turtles shed tears of grief as they leave their newly laid eggs and return to the sea. Leatherback turtles do secrete a saline solution from their eyes, but this is to protect their eyes from the wind and sand while they are on the beach.

Longhouse Living

Longhouses are a traditional form of communal dwelling among the native people of East Malaysia. The entire village is literally housed under one roof. Longhouses are single-story wooden structures constructed on stilts. They are accessible by a notched log that acts as steps. The roofs are traditionally made from woven palm fronds. Within each longhouse is a main hall and many large rooms. The main hall stretches the entire length of the building. This is the communal area, where the villagers gather to socialize and play. Individual families live in the large rooms. The two main tribes in Sarawak that still live in longhouses are the Bidayuh and the Iban.

Each longhouse is headed by a tuai rumah. The title and responsibility that comes with the title are passed on to the first-born male child of the family. If the family does not have a male child, the honor is passed on to the tuai rumah's son-in-law or

Below: **This longhouse in Bavanggazo village, Sabah, was developed as a cultural showcase by the Sabah Tourism Promotion Corporation and the villagers. This has allowed the village to preserve its culture and heritage while generating an income.**

Above: **These Iban people go about their daily chores in a longhouse in Sarawak.**

nephew. The tuai rumah is responsible for the fair division of food and other items among the residents of the longhouse. He also acts as a mediator in solving any problems within the longhouse. Until the early twentieth century, he was also responsible for leading the longhouse warriors to battle. The winning group would cut off the heads of their opponents as trophies. Some of the skulls can still be seen hanging in longhouses today. James Brooke outlawed this practice when he became the first white rajah, or ruler, of Sarawak in 1841.

The main economic activities carried out by longhouse communities include agriculture, hunting, and gathering the produce of the rain forest. Since rice is the staple diet of the native groups, many communities plant rice, also known as hill paddy. They practice shifting cultivation. Today, many of the longhouse inhabitants also sell their wares in the markets of nearby towns and use the money to buy additional supplies for their families. The younger members of these communities may also attend school and move to cities to work when they are older.

SHIFTING CULTIVATION

In shifting cultivation, farmers make a clearing in the forest and plant a crop of paddy, or rice, together with a few other crops, such as tapioca or sweet potato. The crops are harvested at various intervals to ensure the community has a continuous supply of food throughout the year. Once the land loses its fertility, the communities move on.

Melaka

The Malaccan empire was the most important Malay empire in Southeast Asia in the fifteenth century. While there are various accounts about Melaka's early history, most historians attribute its founding to Parameswara, a Sumatran prince. One of the more renowned accounts is a story associated with the naming of Melaka. During one of his hunting trips, Parameswara's hunting dogs cornered a mouse deer. The mouse deer fought for its life and forced the dogs to run away. Believing this was a good omen, Parameswara decided to establish a city there and name it after the tree under which he was sitting. The tree was a melaka tree.

A Successful Port

Melaka's deep and protected harbor was an ideal stopover for ships sailing to and from India and China. It also flourished with traders coming from as far as the Middle East. Besides its geographical advantages, Melaka's success as a port was also

Below: **Once a hive of activity, Melaka River is now a picture of calm.**

due to various policies and strategies implemented by its rulers. They had the support of the *Orang Laut* (OH-rahng LAH-oat), or sea gypsies, who attacked any ship that did not visit the port. In doing so, they ensured the growth of the shipping industry in Melaka. In addition, the rulers also appointed *syahbandars* (SHAH-bahn-dahs) to represent the different ethnic groups that came to Melaka. Since monsoon winds determined the arrival and departure of the traders, underground warehouses were built to protect goods from fire, rain, or theft. Melaka also provided the traders with security within the city limits.

Above: **Christ Church, one of Melaka's many historical buildings, was built by the Dutch in 1753.**

The Fall of Melaka

Melaka's prosperity made it a target for the Portuguese, who wanted to take over the lucrative spice trade. The Portuguese, led by Alfonso d'Albuquerque, succeeded in conquering Melaka in 1511. With the fall of Melaka, the residents of the sultanate fled to other Malay states. Melaka was then ruled by a series of colonial masters until the country's independence in 1957. Today, Melaka is known as the historic city of Malaysia. Portuguese and Dutch influence is still evident in the city's architecture.

P. Ramlee

Ramlee bin Puteh, or P. Ramlee (1929–1973) as he is better known, was perhaps the most popular Malay singer, actor, director, and producer to have graced the Malaysian entertainment industry. He combined the genres and stylistic features of Indian, British, and Japanese film, making his movies unique.

P. Ramlee was born on March 22, 1929, on Pinang. From a young age, he had a talent for singing and acting. During the Japanese occupation in World War II, he enrolled in the Japanese Navy School and learned to play piano, violin, and guitar under a Japanese music teacher. When the war ended, P. Ramlee studied music under a local Malay music teacher.

In 1945, P. Ramlee formed a band that entered the Northern Region Singing Competition. The band placed third. He entered the same competition again in 1946 and 1947, winning second and first place, respectively. Subsequently, a film director from Singapore recognized his talent and offered him a job singing and composing songs for films. In 1948, P. Ramlee went to Singapore

Left: P. Ramlee (*left*), comedian Benny Hill (*middle*), and actress Sarimah (*right*) take a break from acting at the Shaw Brothers' Jalan Ampas studio in Singapore.

Left: P. Ramlee won many awards in his lifetime. He is pictured here with his wife, actress Salmah Ismail, who is affectionately known to the public as Saloma.

to take up the position. Months later, he acted in his first film, *Cinta* (*Love*), as a villain. He continued acting in a number of small roles before he was offered a major role. While working on these movies, P. Ramlee learned as much as he could about making movies by talking to the people around him. In 1955, he acted in his final film, *Hang Tuah,* before moving on to become a director. The first movie he directed, *Penarik Beca* (*Trishaw Puller*), won the best movie and best song awards in a survey conducted by a local magazine. From there, he went on to win many more awards.

In 1964, P. Ramlee left Singapore and went to Kuala Lumpur where he joined Studio Merdeka. There, he produced eighteen more movies. He also continued to compose many songs.

P. Ramlee passed away suddenly in 1973. In his lifetime, he made sixty-one movies, thirty-four of which he directed. The movies he made were enjoyed by all. Today, his movies continue to be shown regularly on television.

The Peranakans

Peranakans are an excellent example of early cross-cultural interactions in Malaysia. The first Peranakans were the offspring of Chinese immigrants who married local Malays in Melaka. It is also recorded that in 1459, a Chinese princess, Hang Li Po, was given in marriage to Sultan Mansur Shah of Melaka. Five hundred Chinese handmaidens accompanied the princess. These handmaidens married local men and had Peranakan children.

A Peranakan man is known as a *baba* (BAH-bah), and a Peranakan woman is known as a *nyonya* (NYOH-nyah). The golden age for Peranakans was during the eighteenth and nineteenth centuries. They were known to be excellent business people and were shrewd and clever in handling business matters. Many Peranakan families made their fortunes at this time, trading spices, timber, tin, and rubber. The wealth of Peranakans was reflected in their homes, which were lavishly decorated and usually contained teak or rosewood furniture.

Above: **This portrait of a baba is dated 1907.**

Left: **A Peranakan family is dressed in Peranakan traditional clothing. Their clothes are a blend of Malay and Chinese styles.**

Above: **This collection of Peranakan accessories was crafted from silver.**

The Peranakan culture was a unique blend of Chinese, Malay, and European cultures. Peranakans observed Chinese traditions and festivals, but their dress was largely influenced by Malay styles. They practiced ancestral worship and celebrated the Chinese New Year. A baba's dress was later also influenced by European styles.

Nyonyas were excellent homemakers. They developed a unique cuisine that blended Malay spices and Chinese methods of cooking. They used coconut milk, *belacan* (ber-LAH-chan), chilies, and spices to flavor their meals. They were also adept at making fine pastries and cakes. Nyonyas also excelled at sewing, embroidery, and beadwork, producing domestic items such as pillow covers, bed hangings, slippers, and other accessories.

The Peranakans were well known for their porcelain tableware and other home artifacts. Porcelain tableware was usually of high quality and custom-made in China. The items had bold and brilliant colors and usually featured phoenixes and peonies. These porcelain pieces were reserved for ceremonial use and are valuable collector's items today.

PERANAKAN WEDDINGS

A Peranakan wedding ceremony used to be an elaborate twelve-day celebration because the people believed that a person remained a child until the day he or she got married. Thus, marriage was a cause for celebration.

61

The Petronas Towers

Recognized as the world's tallest building, the Petronas Towers stand at a height of 1,483 feet (452 m) in the heart of Kuala Lumpur's city center. The building consists of two tapering twin towers, each with eighty-eight floors. Although the next tallest building, the Sears Tower in Chicago, has 110 floors, the Petronas Towers are considered to be the taller building because of the total height of the permanent structure, including a tall spire that stands atop each tower.

An Architectural Feat

The Petronas Towers were constructed over a five-year period and completed in 1996. Occupation of the building began in 1997. The towers were built with a combination of steel and concrete, as well as aluminum and stainless steel for the exterior. A double-decked sky bridge connects the towers at the forty-first and forty-second floors. The sky bridge is 191.6 feet (58.4 m) long, and it took more than three days to put it into place. The bridge is 558 feet (170 m) above street level.

Designed by the American architecture firm Cesar Pelli and Associates, the towers were built as a monument to reflect Kuala Lumpur's prominence as a commercial and cultural center. The high-tech building features high speed double-decked elevators, an advanced building control system to manage and monitor the building's air conditioning, lighting, electricity, and water supply, a superior building security system that includes a closed circuit television system and a photo identification system, as well as a high-level telecommunications system. The architects also incorporated Islamic motifs into the design of the building to represent Malaysia's dominant Islamic culture. The floor plate of each tower is in the shape of an eight-point star. The star is an Islamic motif that symbolizes the spread of Islam. The Petronas Towers is a modern building with a distinct Malaysian identity.

Apart from the offices located in the towers, Petronas Towers also houses one of the largest shopping centers in Malaysia. Other facilities include a concert hall that can seat 864 people, a multimedia conference center, an art gallery, a mosque, and an underground parking lot with 4,500 parking spaces.

Above: **The sky bridge facilitates movement between the towers.**

Putrajaya

A truly modern city ahead of its time, Putrajaya is just 15.5 miles (25 km) from Kuala Lumpur. Together with its twin city, Cyberjaya, Putrajaya forms the nucleus of an ambitious project by the Malaysian government — the Multimedia Super Corridor (MSC). The MSC is designed with advanced infrastructure and equipped with cutting-edge technology to attract world-class multimedia and information technology (IT) companies to Malaysia. Putrajaya is the nation's new administrative center of the federal government.

A Marriage of Technology and Nature

The main concept behind the construction of Putrajaya was to combine technology with nature. Thus, Putrajaya has been developed both as a garden city and an intelligent city. About 40 percent of Putrajaya features lush greenery, lakes, and wetlands for the purpose of conservation, education, and research. As an intelligent city, the entire community within Putrajaya is electronically integrated and linked, such that

Below: **The Perdana Putra Building in Putrajaya houses a number of government offices, including that of the prime minister.**

products and services are available and accessible to anyone anywhere and at anytime. This includes the concept of smart homes, whereby home appliances are fully automated to relieve residents of mundane tasks, and public services can be assessed online from the home, office, or independent kiosks. Commercial buildings are also designed so that they are efficient and cost-effective to run and manage and are environment-friendly.

Above: **The Putra Mosque can accommodate up to 15,000 worshipers at any one time.**

Putrajaya is divided into two main areas — the Core Area and the Periphery Area. These two areas are physically separated by a 988-acre (400-hectare) manmade lake. The Core Area is about 5 square miles (13 square km) and is divided into five precincts. They are the Government Precinct, Mixed Development Precinct, Civic and Cultural Precinct, Commercial Precinct, and Sports and Recreational Precinct.

In contrast, the Periphery Area is a residential area. This area has fourteen residential neighborhoods with a total of 67,000 different housing units to cater to people of all income levels. Most of these neighborhoods feature community and neighborhood centers, places of worship, and parks, in addition to other state-of-the-art public amenities.

Rain Forests

Malaysia's rain forests are among the oldest in the world. They occupy about 47 percent of Malaysia's total land area and can be found both on the lowlands and hills. Plant and animal species thrive because of the region's high rainfall, and many of these species are unique to Malaysia. These rain forests are known to support about 15,000 species of flowering plants, 4,200 species of trees, 800 species of fern, 286 species of birds, 406 species of amphibians and reptiles, and over 100,000 species of insects. Many more species of flora and fauna have yet to be discovered. At present, over a quarter of medicines are derived from plants, and it is believed that the cures for cancer, AIDS, and other illnesses may be found in the rain forest.

Deforestation

Since the mid-1990s, the rate of deforestation in Malaysia's rain forests has been over 2.4 percent per year. This is due to the logging and clearing of land for residential, industrial, and commercial purposes. Increasing population is one of the factors contributing to the clearing of the rain forest. The biggest

Left: **This tropical rain forest on Pulau Pangkor, off the coast of Perak, is thick and green with vegetation.**

ecological threat in Malaysia at present is the building of the Bakun Dam in eastern Sarawak. The dam has been planned as an additional source of electricity for the nation. Some ten thousand indigenous people have already been resettled to make way for the building of the dam.

Above: **Large areas of rain forest in Sarawak have been cleared to make way for the Bakun Dam.**

Protecting the Rain Forest

The Malaysian government is taking steps to ensure that not all the nation's rain forests will be destroyed. The government is establishing nature reserves and protecting them by passing legislation. Malaysia has also adopted the principle of sustainable development, which uses natural resources at a rate that will not cause any damage to the environment. This includes reducing the level of pollution generated by industries and development and establishing buffer zones between forests and human settlements. While these are positive steps, it remains to be seen whether the concept of sustainable development will be successful in preserving the rain forests of Malaysia.

BAKUN DAM

Work on the Bakun Dam is being carried out in the Sarawakian rain forest. There has been much opposition to the project because of the threat to the rain forest, and, as a result, it may be scaled down, but the outcome is uncertain at present .

Rubber and Oil palm

Rubber was first introduced into Malaya in 1877, but it was in the mid-1890s that it was first exploited as a commercial crop. The expansion of the automobile industry in the early 1900s caused demand for rubber to increase and the prices to rise. During this period, the number of rubber plantations in Malaya grew sharply. The majority of the rubber estates were cultivated in the states along the western coast. This was due to the presence of an infrastructure of railway lines, road networks, and ports that was already developed for the tin mining industry. The government further encouraged rubber cultivation by allocating more land for rubber estates and offering favorable terms for the flow of capital and the employment of labor. By 1916, rubber had become Malaya's chief export earner. Today, Malaysia is one of the world's top rubber producers.

Above: **To facilitate the work of rubber tappers, rubber trees are grown in neat rows.**

Left: **A worker hangs out rubber sheets to dry before they are smoked. The process of smoking stabilizes the rubber before it is sent to manufacturers.**

THE FATHER OF RUBBER

English botanist Henry Nicholas Ridley (1855-1956) was known as the Father of Rubber. He encouraged planters in Malaysia to cultivate rubber as a crop. He also introduced modern rubber tapping methods to them.

Left: **Oil palms are most productive between the ages of three and seven.**

When the price of rubber fell in the 1920s, planters turned to another crop, oil palm. Although the commercial planting of oil palm was first done in 1917 in Malaya, it was overshadowed by the success of rubber. Malaya's tropical climate and soils favored the cultivation of oil palm. Nevertheless, expertise was needed in cultivating the plant and in processing the oil. Thus, only the larger plantations with the financial ability took to cultivating oil palm.

Oil from the oil palm is a versatile source of edible and non-edible fats. Palm oil is used in the production of cooking oil, ice cream, and margarine, as well as the manufacture of candles, detergents, hair conditioners, and paints. The many uses of oil palm make it a valuable commercial crop for Malaysia. Today, Malaysia accounts for about half of the world's production of palm oil.

Above: **These red oil palm fruit are ripe and ready for harvesting. The fruit is pressed to release the palm oil.**

Sepak Takraw

Sepak takraw is Malaysia's national sport. It is a game that requires an amazing amount of coordination and agility. Played by two *regu* (REE-goo), or three-player teams, the game utilizes a court similar to a badminton court. The ball is woven of natural rattan or synthetic fiber and has twelve holes. The game is similar in principle to volleyball, with a few exceptions. The players are not to use their hands to touch the ball. Each player is allowed to kick the ball only once before passing it over to the opponent's side of the court. The game is played in sets of three. The first team to score fifteen points wins a set. The team that wins two sets wins the match. If there is a tie, an additional set is played to determine the winning team.

Sepak means "kick" in Malay, and *takraw* means "ball" in Thai. Records show the game was enjoyed in Southeast Asia as early as the eleventh century. In Malaysia, the traditional

Above: **In tournaments, the modern sepak takraw ball is used.**

Left: **The Malaysian sepak takraw team (*in blue jerseys*) plays against the Indonesian team (*in red jerseys*) at the 2001 SEA Games in Kuala Lumpur.**

version of sepak takraw was played by as many as twelve people standing in a circle who kept the ball in the air without using their hands. It was popular among the royals as well as the common people. This traditional version of the game is still popular in Malaysia today.

Above: **The Malaysian sepak takraw team (*in yellow jerseys*) serves the ball at the Sepak Takraw World Cup 2002 held in Singapore.**

The modern version of sepak takraw was gradually introduced in the early twentieth century. One of the biggest developments in sepak takraw was the invention of the spiking maneuver. As in volleyball, spiking involves a player hitting the ball into the opponent's side of the court at great speed. In sepak takraw, the player gains momentum by running up to the net and doing a back flip before kicking the ball over the net while in mid-air.

Sepak takraw are medal events in the Southeast Asian (SEA) Games and Asian Games. Before 1998, however, little was known about the game outside Asia. In that year, the game was introduced as a demonstration sport in the Commonwealth Games held in Kuala Lumpur. It is now played in over twenty countries worldwide.

Wayang Kulit

Wayang kulit, or shadow puppet theater, is the oldest form of theater in Malaysia. Although the exact origins of the art are unclear, it is said that wayang kulit was brought to Malaysia from the island of Java, Indonesia, hundreds of years ago. It is now part of Malaysian heritage. Wayang kulit is popular on the eastern coast of Peninsular Malaysia, especially in the states of Kelantan and Terengganu and in the northern states of Kedah and Perlis.

Wayang kulit puppets are two-dimensional and have movable arms and legs, which are mounted on bamboo sticks. Their features are usually highly exaggerated. The puppets are traditionally handcrafted from buffalo or goat parchment, but cardboard and scrap metal are also used today. Color is added using traditional pigments, but some puppets are also painted with store-bought paint.

Wayang kulit troupes traditionally perform plays adapted from the Hindu epics, consisting of romantic and supernatural tales. The most popular adaptations are legends from the

Left: **These shadow puppets are lovers in a romantic tale.**

Above: **The tok dalang and his orchestra work behind the scenes of a shadow puppet show.**

Ramayana and *Mahabharata* epics. Today, plays based on current issues are also performed.

Before the show begins, a screen of white cotton is erected. A bright electric bulb or oil lamp is used as a light source to cast shadows on the screen. In olden times, the light source was a small fire. The master of the show, or *tok dalang* (TOHK DAH-lang), sits behind the screen and controls the movements of the puppets. He is in charge of the entire performance, from the movements of the puppets, to the narration of the story, to the dialogue between the puppets. Some performances have as many as forty-five different characters and the tok dalang handles them all on his own. This master puppeteer and storyteller also needs to be physically strong since a wayang kulit performance can stretch up to nine hours.

The wayang kulit performance is accompanied by a small orchestra, which consists mainly of percussion instruments. It is also the tok dalang's task to compose the music for the performance. As the orchestra plays, the tok dalang uses his voice to create additional drama and suspense.

RELATIONS WITH NORTH AMERICA

Until recently, North America's ties with Malaysia were limited, though the relationship was one of goodwill. This is because Malaysia is a relatively young country. During his administration (1963–1969), American president Lyndon B. Johnson visited Malaysia. He was the first American president to visit the country, and he remains the only one at present. Malaysia's economy and importance in the global arena are, however, improving greatly. Today, the United States and Canada share close diplomatic and economic ties with Malaysia. Both the

Opposite: **Restaurants serving American-style meals, such as Planet Hollywood in Kuala Lumpur, are becoming increasingly common in Malaysia.**

United States and Canada are Malaysia's leading economic partners and export markets. North America is also Malaysia's largest source of foreign direct investment.

Relations between North America and Malaysia have been given more opportunity for growth with Malaysia's active membership in the U.N., the U.N. Security Council, the Asia-Pacific Economic Cooperation Forum (APEC), ASEAN Dialogue Partners, the ASEAN Regional Forum (ARF), the World Trade Organization (WTO), and the Commonwealth of Nations, of which Canada is a member.

Above: **A group of North American tourists enjoy a trishaw ride around the streets of Melaka.**

Military Ties

Apart from diplomatic and economic relations, Malaysia has also established defense and security ties with the United States in the form of joint exercises between the respective armed forces. These exercises are implemented under the International Military Education and Training program (IMET) and the Bilateral Training and Consultative Group (BITACG) program. These programs help strengthen the military relations between the two countries and allow the Malaysian military to become more familiar with the equipment and management techniques of the U.S. military.

U.S. Pacific Command

The United States established the U.S. Pacific Command on January 1, 1947, with the intention of fostering positive relationships, enhancing security, and detering aggression in the Asia Pacific region. In September 2001, the U.S. Army and the Malaysian Army cohosted the 25th Pacific Armies Management Seminar (PAMS XXV), which was held in Kuala Lumpur. It was a multinational military seminar where senior officers from Asia Pacific's ground forces gathered to exchange views and ideas.

Left: Lieutenant General E.P. Smith (*right*) of the U.S. Army and Lieutenant General Dato' Pahlawan Khairuddin bin Mat Yusof (*left*) of the Malaysian Army shake hands during the opening of the 25th Annual Pacific Armies Management Seminar in September 2001.

Left: **On May 14, 2002, in the White House in Washington, D.C., U.S. president George W. Bush (*right*) welcomed Malaysian prime minister Dr. Mahathir bin Mohamad (*left*) as an ally in the fight against terrorism.**

Peace

Malaysia is outspoken on international and military issues. When the United States imposed sanctions on Iraq in 1990 and on Afghanistan in 2001, Malaysia voiced its protest. Malaysia's occasional protests against U.S. policies do not indicate anti-American feeling. The Malaysian government simply prefers nonviolent solutions to measures involving a threat to lives. This peaceful attitude is reflected in Malaysia's involvement in the formation of the Zone of Peace, Freedom, and Neutrality (ZOPFAN) among the ASEAN countries during the Cold War, a post–World War II conflict between the United States and the former Soviet Union. The countries participating in the ZOPFAN did not take sides in the Cold War.

Malaysia also condemned the Iraqi invasion of Kuwait in 1990 and the September 11, 2001 terrorist attacks on the United States. After the attacks, Malaysia pledged to work with the United States against terrorism and provided the United States with key information about Islamic militants and their activities. Malaysia has arrested more than sixty people suspected to be linked to the Al-Qaeda network, a terrorist organization believed to be behind the September 11, 2001 terrorist attacks. Malaysia's stand against terrorism has made it an important ally to the United States and strengthened the political ties between them.

Human Rights and Democracy

Malaysia has been under considerable scrutiny for its human rights practices since 1998, when Malaysia's former deputy prime minister Anwar Ibrahim was arrested in what was believed to be a politically motivated move. During his imprisonment and while awaiting trial, Anwar was ill-treated and abused. Immense international pressure and strong protest from human rights groups in the United States resulted in the then Malaysian chief of police being convicted of the abuse and imprisoned. Apart from this issue, the United States also protests the severe censorship of the Malaysian press by the Malaysian government.

Below: **U.N. Secretary-General Kofi Annan (*left*) meets with Malaysian prime minister Dr. Mahathir bin Mohamad (*right*) on his official visit to Malaysia on December 16, 1997.**

An example of this is Malaysia's restrictions on the Harakah newspaper, the publication of a political opposition party in Malaysia. In March 2000, the government limited the Harakah newspaper to publish only two editions a month instead of two editions a week. Among those who protested the move was the Committee to Protect Journalists (CPJ), a group based in New York. The CPJ believed that the move to cut down the frequency of the publication was due to the newspaper's growing circulation and readership.

While Malaysia's ideas about human rights and democracy may differ from those of the United States and Canada, relations between the nations remain friendly and cooperative.

Scientific Collaboration

From 1997 to 1999, Malaysia faced a terrible crisis. A viral infection was spreading rapidly among the workers at pig farms throughout the country and causing human fatalities. The disease was initially believed to be Japanese encephalitis (JE), a disease transmitted by mosquitoes. In 1999, the Department of Medical Microbiology at the University of Malaya isolated the virus and brought it to the Arbovirus Research Center, Center for Disease Control (CDC) in Fort Collins, Colorado. Scientists from the United States, Australia, and Japan worked with the scientists from Malaysia to analyze the virus and understand more about

the disease. The virus was found to be related to the Hendra virus. It was named Nipah, after Kampung Baru Sungai Nipah in the western Malaysian state of Negeri Sembilan, where it was first detected. The virus is believed to be transmitted from infected pigs to humans through direct contact. The scientists continued to conduct tests and monitor the situation to help control and eradicate the disease.

About 261 persons were affected by the Nipah virus, 103 of whom died from the infection. The pig farming industry in Malaysia has been drastically affected by the outbreak, but the situation is now under control, thanks to the collaboration between the CDC and the Malaysian authorities.

Above: **Regular and intensive chemical fogging exercises were conducted at pig farms, such as this one in Seremban, to reduce the mosquito population. At that time, the virus was believed to have been spread by mosquitoes.**

Malaysian-U.S. Ties

The United States and Malaysia enjoy good cultural and professional ties. Organizations, such as the American Association of Malaysia (AAM), the Malaysian American Society (MAS), and the Malaysian Professional and Business Association (MPBA), promote goodwill and understanding between people of Malaysia and the United States.

The AAM is a nonprofit organization that provides assistance to Americans living and working in Malaysia. Started in Kuala Lumpur in 1961, its key role is to help U.S. expatriates and students settle into their new lifestyle in Malaysia while helping them keep in touch with home. The organization also works with charities in Malaysia and provides information to Malaysians who are interested in learning more about the opportunities available in the United States.

CANADA'S RELATIONS WITH MALAYSIA

Since the 1950s, the relationship between Canada and Malaysia has been predominantly in the area of development assistance — under the Colombo Plan, then later by means of the Canadian International Development Agency (CIDA). With Malaysia's economic progress in recent years, however, the relationship between the two countries is gradually becoming one of economic and political cooperation.

Left: The golden arches of McDonald's are a common sight in Malaysia's larger cities.

Left: Microsoft's chairman and chief software architect Bill Gates addresses the audience at a talk on the "Connected Community" held in Kuala Lumpur on March 18, 1998.

Like the AAM, the MAS was established in the 1960s in Kuala Lumpur. With a membership that includes prominent Malaysian personalities and members of the American Embassy, the MAS provides a political and economic link with the United States. It also has a presence in Washington, D.C. Some of the largest contributions of the organization include the establishment of trade relations and the maintenance of closer diplomatic ties between the two countries.

The MPBA was founded by a group of Malaysian professionals living in the San Francisco Bay Area in 1992. Headquartered in San Francisco, the MPBA's main objective is to establish a contact point for Malaysian professionals living in North America. It also works to publicize investment and business opportunities available in Malaysia while providing opportunities for members to continue their education through workshops and seminars.

Microsoft and the MSC

When the MSC (Multimedia Super Corridor) was first launched in 1996, it aimed to attract the best IT (information technology) companies to Malaysia. To ensure the success of the MSC, an International Advisory Panel of leading IT experts was set up. One of the members of this panel is Bill Gates, the chairman and Chief Software Architect of Microsoft Corporation.

MICROSOFT KNOWLEDGE CAPITAL CENTRE (MKCC)

To further contribute to the MSC project, Microsoft Corporation has also established a subsidiary company, MKCC. Based in Malaysia, the aim of the MKCC is to provide local software developers, vendors, and other business people with the necessary skills, technology, training, expertise, and innovation to develop and produce quality products and services to stay relevant and compete in the information age.

Malaysians Abroad

Attracted by opportunities available for the education of their children and by the conveniences available in developed nations such as the United States and Canada, a number of Malaysians choose to live abroad.

Many young Malaysians choose to study overseas. They complete an undergraduate degree in a university abroad and then return to Malaysia to work. Organizations such as the Malaysian American Commission on Educational Exchange (MACEE) help students with their university and visa applications to the United States. This assistance has made the application process much easier and thus increased the number of applicants. Easy access to information through the Internet has also helped Malaysian students do research on universities and opportunities in the United States and Canada.

Many private colleges have emerged in Malaysia. These colleges offer diploma and pre-university programs affiliated with universities in the United States and Canada. These colleges also offer students the option to do part of their education in Malaysia and the other part abroad.

Left: **The members of the Purdue University Malaysian Students Association outside the Engineering Mall, Purdue University, West Lafayette campus, Indiana, April, 2002.**

American Popular Culture

The North American entertainment industry has had a big influence on Malaysia. Movies from Hollywood are mainstream entertainment for Malaysians of all ages. North American television shows on Malaysian television also have a large viewership. The popularity of these styles of entertainment has influenced local filmmakers and producers in their own film production techniques and considerations. Hollywood-style elements are increasingly being incorporated into local television shows and movies.

American music, such as rap, rock, and rhythm and blues, has found a large following in Malaysia. Many North American artistes make Kuala Lumpur one of their performing venues when touring Asia. The list of celebrities who have given concerts in Malaysia includes Michael Jackson, Hootie and the Blowfish, and the Backstreet Boys.

Above: **Hollywood films draw crowds to movie theaters in Malaysia.**

Hollywood and Malaysia

The combination of Malaysia's natural beauty, convenient geographical location, modern infrastructure, and exotic culture has helped make Malaysia an attractive filming location for many foreign moviemakers, including Hollywood directors.

Two successful feature films were shot by Twentieth Century Fox Productions in Malaysia — *Entrapment* (1999), starring Sean Connery and Catherine Zeta-Jones, and *Anna and the King* (1999), with Jodie Foster and Chow Yun Fatt. The Petronas Towers in Kuala Lumpur were featured in *Entrapment*, and *Anna and the King* was shot in various locations throughout Penang, Langkawi, and Perak.

While Malaysia attempts to attract foreign filmmakers into the country, Malaysian talents have gone abroad to pursue their careers in Hollywood. Malaysian-born actress Michelle Yeoh played a major role in the 1997 James Bond movie *Tomorrow Never Dies*. She also starred in *Crouching Tiger, Hidden Dragon* (2000), which won four Academy Awards in 2001.

Below: **Malaysia was chosen as the filming location for *Anna and the King*.**

Left: **Malaysian actress Michelle Yeoh acts in a scene from the hit movie *Crouching Tiger, Hidden Dragon*.**

E-Village

Malaysia has invested large sums of money to set up a film production studio to cater to future movie projects filmed within the country. Similar to the concept of Universal Studios, the ongoing project is known as E-Village, or Entertainment Village. E-Village stands on a 3.16-square-mile (8.2-square-km) site located near Cyberjaya and the MSC. The project is being built in three phases, and Phase One opened in 2000. The entire project is due to be completed in 2007. When complete, E-Village will be the largest studio and theme park in Asia. It will be equipped with the best film production resources and cutting-edge technology to attract foreign filmmakers, especially those from the U.S. film industry.

Survivor in Malaysia

The first season of *Survivor*, the reality-based television show on the U.S. CBS network, was filmed in Malaysia on Pulau Tiga. The island lies 6 miles (10 km) off the coast of Sabah. Due to the success of the show, the remote island, which was virtually unknown before, is now a household name in the United States. Malaysia hopes to capitalize on the success of the *Survivor* series to turn the quiet Pulau Tiga Resort into a bustling tourist destination, where vacationers can take part in *Survivor*-like challenges. Proceeds from the show have been used to fund the construction of new facilities on the island.

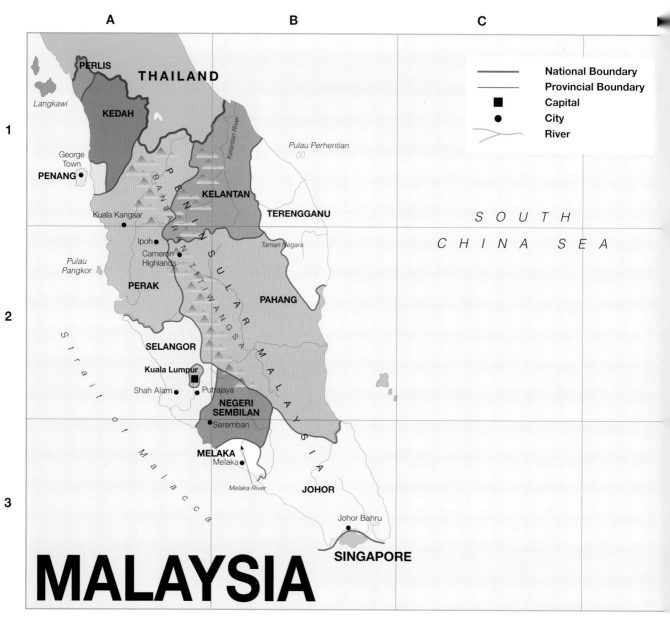

MALAYSIA

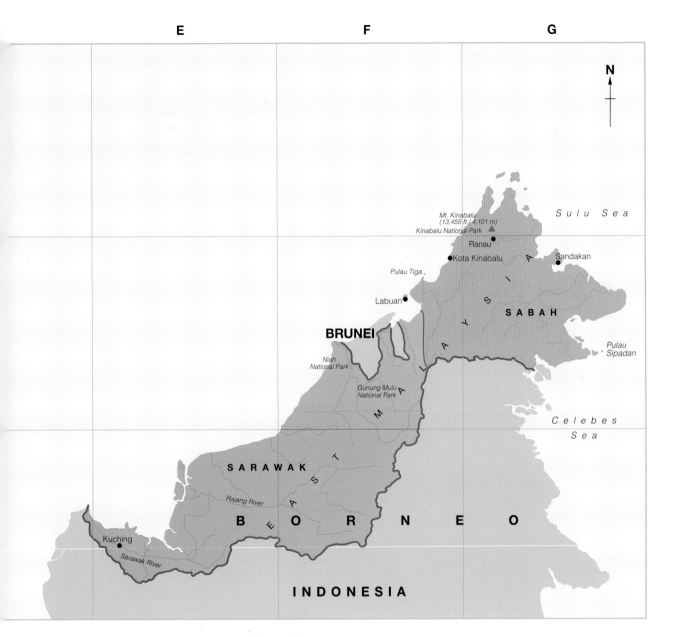

E F G

N

Sulu Sea

Mt. Kinabalu
(13,455 ft / 4,101 m)
Kinabalu National Park ▲

● Ranau

● Kota Kinabalu

● Sandakan

Pulau Tiga

Labuan ●

BRUNEI

M A L A Y S I A

S A B A H

*Pulau
Sipadan*

*Niah
National Park*

*Gunung Mulu
National Park*

*Celebes
Sea*

S A R A W A K

Rajang River

B **O** **R** **N** **E** **O**

E A S T

Kuching ●

Sarawak River

I N D O N E S I A

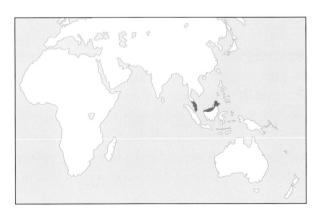

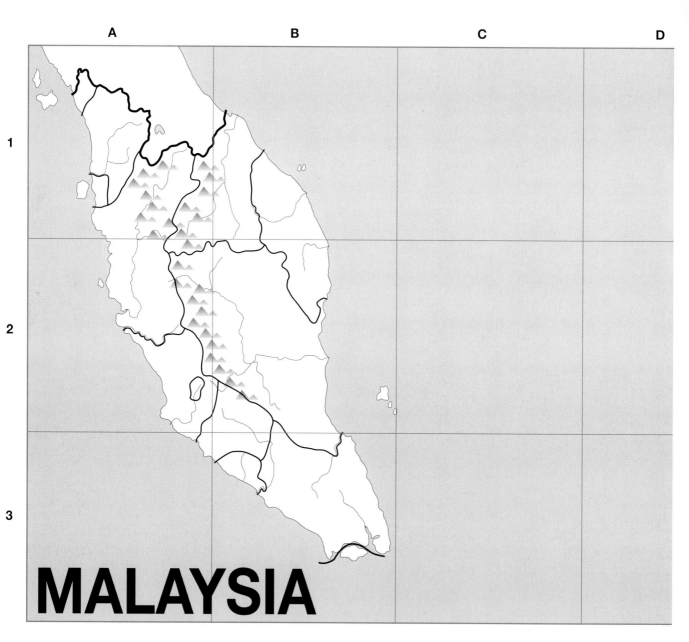

MALAYSIA

How Is Your Geography?

Learning to identify the main geographical areas and points
of a country can be challenging. Although it may seem difficult
at first to memorize the locations and spellings of major cities
or the names of mountain ranges, rivers, deserts, lakes, and
other prominent physical features, the end result of this effort
can be very rewarding. Places you previously did not know
existed will suddenly come to life when referred to in
world news, whether in newspapers, television reports,

other books and reference sources, or on the Internet. This
knowledge will make you feel a bit closer to the rest of the world,
with its fascinating variety of cultures and physical geography.

Used in a classroom setting, the instructor can make duplicates of
this map using a copy machine. (PLEASE DO NOT WRITE IN
THIS BOOK!) Students can then fill in any requested information
on their individual map copies. Used one-on-one, the student can
also make copies of the map on a copy machine and use them as a
study tool. The student can practice identifying place names and
geographical features on his or her own.

Malaysia at a Glance

Official Name	Malaysia
Capital	Kuala Lumpur
States	Johor, Kedah, Kelantan, Melaka, Negeri Sembilan, Pahang, Penang, Perak, Perlis, Sabah, Sarawak, Selangor, Terengganu
Federal Territories	Kuala Lumpur, Labuan, Putrajaya
Official Languages	Bahasa Melayu
Population	22,229,040 (July 2001 estimate)
Land Area	127,317 square miles (329,750 square km)
Highest Point	Mount Kinabalu 13,455 feet (4,101 m)
Ethnic Groups	Malay and other indigenous 58%, Chinese 27%, Indian 8%, others 7% (2000)
Major Religions	Buddhism, Christianity, Hinduism, Islam, Sikhism, Taoism
Important Holidays	Chinese New Year (January/February)
	Thaipusam (January/February)
	Hari Raya Haji (March)
	Vesak Day (May)
	National Day (August 31)
	Deepavali (October/November)
	Christmas (December 25)
	Hari Raya Aidilfitri (December/January)
Major Exports	Chemicals, electronic equipment, palm oil, petroleum and liquefied natural gas, rubber, textiles, wood and wood products
Major Imports	Chemicals, food, fuel, lubricants, machinery and transportation equipment
Currency	Malaysian Ringgit (MYR 3.8 = U.S. $1 as of 2002)

Opposite: **This dancer is dressed in a colorful costume at a national day parade performance.**

Glossary

Malay Vocabulary

adat (ah-DUT): traditions and customary laws.

Aslian (AS-lee-an): the collective word for the languages of the Orang Asli.

ayam goreng (AH-yum GO-rehng): a dish of deep fried chicken and rice.

baba (BAH-bah): a male Peranakan.

Bahasa Melayu (bah-HAA-sah MUH-lah-yoo): the Malay language.

baju Melayu (BAH-joo MUH-lah-yoo): Malay-style clothing.

batik (bah-TEEK): a traditional Malay dyed cloth.

belacan (ber-LAH-chan): a dried shrimp paste, commonly used in Malay cooking.

bertam (ber-TAM): a type of palm.

bumiputera (boo-mih-poo-TRAH): people of ethnic Malay origin.

congkak (CHONG-kak): an indoor Malay game.

gasing (GAH-sing): a giant top.

Hari Raya Aidilfitri (HAH-ree RYE-ah ih-dih-FIT-rih): an Islamic festival that celebrates the end of the fasting month.

Hari Raya Haji (HAH-ree RYE-ah HAH-jee): an Islamic festival that marks the start of the pilgrimage season.

Hari Raya Puasa (HAH-ree RYE-ah PWAH-sah): another name for Hari Raya Aidilfitri.

kapitan (kah-pee-TAN): the head of a Chinese community.

ketua kampong (kuh-TOO-ah kam-PUNG): the head of the village.

ketupat (KUH-too-paht): a rice cake cooked in woven palm leaves.

madrasah (mah-DRAH-sah): a private Islam school.

mak yong (MAK yong): a theatrical dance.

mengkuang (meng-KOO-ang): a type of leaf used for weaving mats.

nasi lemak (NAH-see ler-MAHK): a Malay dish of rice cooked in coconut milk and eaten with fried anchovies, egg, and a sweet chili paste.

ngajat (naa-JAT): a dance of the Iban.

nyonya (NYOH-nyah): a female Peranakan.

Orang Asli (OH-rahng AS-lee): the indigenous people of Malaysia.

Orang Laut (OH-rahng LAH-oat): people of the sea or sea gypsies.

pandan (pan-DAHN): a fragrant leaf used for cooking and weaving.

pantun (pahn-TUHN): poetry with four or more rhyming verses.

Peranakans (puh-RAH-nah-KAHNS): people of mixed Malay and Chinese ancestry.

regu (REE-goo): team.

rendang (RUHNG-dahng): a rich and spicy meat curry.

roti canai (ROH-tee CHA-nai): an Indian pancake served with curry.

sajak (sah-JAK): free verse.

satay (SAH-tay): skewered charcoal-cooked meat, served with peanut sauce.

sepak takraw (seh-PAHK TAHK-raw): a sport played using a rattan ball.

surau (soo-RAU): a Muslim prayer room.

syahbandars (SHAH-bahn-dahs): harbor masters.

syair (sha-IR): poetry that is usually sung.

Syariah (SHAH-ree-ah): Islamic law.

Syawal (SYE-waw): the tenth month of the Islamic calendar.

tok dalang (TOHK DAH-lang): the master puppeteer in a shadow puppet show.

tuai rumah (too-AI roo-MAH): the head of the longhouse.

wau bulan (WOW BOO-lan): a type of Malay kite with a crescent-shaped tail.

wayang kulit (WAH-yang koo-LIT): traditional shadow puppetry.

Yang Dipertuan Agong (YANG dee-puh-TU-an ah-GUNG): the paramount ruler and king of Malaysia.

zakat (ZAH-kaht): a compulsory monetary payment collected to help the poor and to further the cause of Islam.

zapin (za-PEEN): a form of Malay dance.

Tamil (Indian) Vocabulary

Deepavali (dee-PAH-vah-lee): the Hindu festival of lights that celebrates the triumph of good over evil.

kavadi (KAH-vah-dee): a large framework worn by Hindu devotees during the Thaipusam festival.

Thaipusam (TIE-poo-sahm): a Hindu festival of endurance and self-sacrifice.

Mandarin (Chinese) Vocabulary

chap goh mei (CHAP goh meh): a Hokkien term meaning "fifteenth day."

char kway teow (CHAH kway tee-ow): a dish of flat rice noodles stir-fried in black sauce.

English Vocabulary

activist: a person who takes aggressive action to achieve political goals.

archaeological: relating to the study of ancient peoples.

buttress: the flared trunk of tropical trees.

carapace: a hard, bony outer covering.

coalition: an alliance or union.

cohesive: closely integrated.

dehydration: an excessive loss of fluids.

exemptions: not subject to laws or rules.

genre: a category of literary composition.

indigenous: originating in or characteristic of a particular region or country.

infrastructure: a system of facilities and services serving a region or country.

lobbied: to have conducted activities to influence the opinion of public officials for or against a specific cause.

matriarchal: ruled by a woman.

monsoon: a seasonal wind that brings heavy rainfall to Asia.

nomadic: roaming from place to place.

ousted: to have removed by force.

paddy: rice, or the field where it is grown.

paramount: having the highest authority.

patriarchal: ruled by a man.

pewter: an alloy of tin used for tableware.

pollinate: to transfer pollen from an anther to the stigma of a flower.

reincarnation: the rebirth of a soul into a human body.

shamanism: a belief in powerful spirits who are responsive only to shamans.

sovereign: self-governing; independent.

sultanate: the territory ruled by a sultan.

sultans: rulers.

taxonomic: related to the classification of organisms.

More Books to Read

Malaysia. Jonathon Rowell (Raintree/Steck-Vaughn)

Malaysia. Cultures of the World series. Heidi Munan (Benchmark Books)

Malaysia: Heart of Southeast Asia: Photographs by 46 of the World's Finest Photographers. Gavin Young (Charles E Tuttle)

Malaysia in Pictures. Visual Geography series. (Lerner)

Michelle Yeoh. Martial Arts Masters series. Nancy Stair (Rosen Publishing)

The National Parks and Other Wild Places of Malaysia. Gerald S. Cubitt and World Wildlife Fund Malaysia (New Holland/Struik)

The Petronas Towers: The World's Tallest Building. Mark Thomas (Rosen Publishing)

A Photographic Guide to Snakes and Other Reptiles of Peninsular Malaysia, Singapore, and Thailand. Merel J. Cox, Peter Paul van Dijk, Jarujin Nabhitabhata, and Kumthorn Thirakhupt (Ralph Curtis)

A Photographic Guide to the Birds of Peninsular Malaysia and Singapore. G. W. H. Davison and Chew Yen Fook (Ralph Curtis)

Southern and Eastern Asia. World in Maps series. Martyn Bramwell (Lerner)

Videos

Malaysia. (Education 2000)

Skyscrapers. Super Structures of the World series. (Unapix)

Web Sites

www.fascinatingmalaysia.com

www.tourism.gov.my

www.visitmalaysia.com

www.wwfmalaysia.org

Due to the dynamic nature of the Internet, some web sites stay current longer than others. To find additional web sites, use a reliable search engine with one or more of the following keywords to help you locate information about Malaysia. Keywords: *Kinabalu, Kuala Lumpur, Mahathir, Putrajaya, Sabah, Sarawak, Taman Negara.*

Index